WHAT EVERY

NEEDS TO KNOW

WHAT EVERY
Groom
NEEDS TO KNOW

THE MOST IMPORTANT YEAR
IN A MAN'S LIFE

ROBERT WOLGEMUTH & MARK DEVRIES

ZONDERVAN®

ZONDERVAN.com/
AUTHORTRACKER
follow your favorite authors

ZONDERVAN

What Every Groom Needs to Know
Copyright © 2012 by Robert D. Wolgemuth and Mark DeVries
Revised and expanded from *The Most Important Year in a Man's Life*.
Copyright © 2003 by Robert D. Wolgemuth and Mark DeVries.

This title is also available as a Zondervan ebook.
Visit www.zondervan.com/ebooks.

This title is also available in a Zondervan audio edition.
Visit www.zondervan.com/fm.

Requests for information should be addressed to:

Zondervan, *Grand Rapids, Michigan 49530*

ISBN 978-0-310-31359-5

Published in association with the literary agency of Ann Spangler & Company, 1420
Pontiac Road SE, Grand Rapids, MI 49506.

Cover photography: Paul Shippert Photography
Interior design: Cindy Davis
TRADE decoration: IKEA

Printed in the United States of America

12 13 14 15 16 17 18 19 /DCI/ 20 19 18 17 16 15 14 13 12 11 10 9 8 7 6 5 4 3 2 1

CONTENTS

INTRODUCTION

I t doesn't matter how you happened to get a copy of this book. It may have been a wedding gift to you and your bride; it may have been given to you by a friend, a minister, or a professional counselor. What matters, really, in the end is that you're here.

You may be eager to dive in and learn everything you can about having a great marriage. You may forego meals and sporting events until you get the whole way through because you're so excited. Or maybe not.

SOME PERSPECTIVE

When I opened the huge box I had just wrestled from the trunk of my car and set it on the garage floor, there was a piece of paper lying on top of all the unassembled pieces. "Warning: Improper Assembly May Cause Serious Injury" was printed on a piece of inescapable, iridescent lime-green paper.

My wife, Bobbie, and I had just bought one of those gigantic gas grills. I enjoyed barbecuing but decided that I had coaxed my last pile of smoldering charcoal briquettes. I needed gas!

The outside of the box had alerted me that there was "Some Assembly Required." But when I opened the crate and saw the lime-green warning, I became very serious about following the instructions. It was the words *may cause serious injury* that did it. Envisioning raw steaks on the grill and a well-done chef was not a pretty thing.

Your marriage license should have included a similar notice printed on loud paper: "Warning: Not Paying Attention to the *First Year of Marriage* May Result in Serious Lifelong Consequences—Unhappiness Like You Can't Imagine."

So you can think of this book as an assembly manual for your marriage—much easier to follow than the one included with the gas grill.

WHO ARE THESE PEOPLE AND WHAT ARE THEY TRYING TO DO?

This book and the companion book, *What Every Bride Needs to Know*, are the result of the collaborative effort of two couples—Mark and Susan DeVries, and Bobbie and me, Robert Wolgemuth. Mark and Susan have been our close friends for many years. Our daughters, Missy and Julie, grew up with Mark and Susan, who were their youth leaders and mentors. Eventually our daughters both worked with them as volunteers in youth ministry.

As a pastor, Mark has counseled hundreds of engaged couples (sometimes with Susan, sometimes by himself), including our two daughters and their fiancés, Jon and Christopher. Seeing firsthand the effect of Mark and Susan's premarital counseling with our own children, we wanted to make these crucial insights available to others—people like you who may never have the chance to meet Mark and Susan.

Being a lay minister and Bible teacher for over forty years has also allowed me to be involved with many couples who have dealt with marital challenges. And I've come to a single conclusion: There is no more important human quest than building exceptional marriages. The principles you will soon read about were not learned in a classroom but through our own experience, particularly the multitude of mistakes we've made during the combined total of almost seven decades of our own marriages.

These two books have matching themes but contain quite different material. In this book, *What Every Groom Needs to Know*, Mark and I are speaking on the "men's side"; in *What Every Bride Needs to Know*, Susan and Bobbie are speaking on the "women's side." In this book, you will hear my voice throughout; in *What Every Bride Needs to Know*, your wife will hear Susan's. But Mark and Bobbie—whose voices you will not hear but whose names you will often see—have been at the heart of the development and the actual writing of both books from day one.

WHAT AM I SUPPOSED TO DO WITH THIS BOOK?

We want you to know from the outset that this is not a book to help you understand "the ordinary woman"—we realize that the woman you have married is not ordinary. This is a book to help you accomplish your mission of becoming an expert on how to bring happiness to just one woman and, in turn, enjoy the benefits of a great partnership.

Though different couples will approach these books in different ways, here's a process that can help you take what you are learning in these chapters and apply it to the end that you and your spouse will know and enjoy each other more:

Feel Free to Sneak: Once the first drafts of the manuscripts for these books were complete, we presented copies to several volunteers from our Sunday school class for their reading and evaluation. We found that wives had a funny habit of reading the men's book. And every now and then, even the most reading-resistant man would snoop around in the women's book. That's good. Some of the best interaction you will experience will come when you and your wife read portions from each other's book and then say, "That's me," or, "I'm not like that at all!"

Ask the Expert: There will likely be things you read about "women in general" that just aren't true about your wife. When you run across those things, ask your wife questions such as "Is this really what you think?" and "Is this true for you?"

Be the Expert: Even if you've only been married for a few weeks, your wife may already be struggling. Some researchers estimate that as many as 90 percent of brides experience some depression in their first year of marriage.[1] The more your bride has the chance to feel understood, to hear your reaction to what you're reading, the more quickly you'll see the fog of uncertainty lift.

A FEW MORE THINGS

The subtitle for this book is true for men who choose to marry. However, if the first year of marriage were the most important year in *every* man's life, a person of no less stature than Jesus would have missed "the most important year" in his life. Because you and I *have* married and because the first year of marriage *is* so critical in shaping our future, we are convinced that the subtitle *The Most Important Year in a Man's Life* best conveys the heart of our message.

Some long-married couples who have reviewed these books have asked, "Is it too late for us to have the most important year?" Actually, no. If after several years of marriage you and your wife are willing to wake up to your need to invest in your relationship in a whole new way, it is *not* too late. So whether you've been married for thirty days or for thirty years, we invite you to let this next year be *the most important year* of your life.

Just a final note: The stories you are about to read are true. In most cases, the names and the circumstances have been changed to mask the identity of those whose stories we are telling.

Robert Wolgemuth   *Mark DeVries*
Orlando, Florida   *Nashville, Tennessee*

1

THE MOST IMPORTANT YEAR: BRINGING HAPPINESS TO YOUR WIFE

If trying hard was the key to a healthy marriage, most couples would find themselves in the Healthy Marriage Hall of Fame.

JEFF VAN VONDEREN, *FAMILIES WHERE GRACE IS IN PLACE*

The coach had seen enough. He called for a time-out and motioned his quarterback over to the sidelines. Something horrible was going on out there, and the quarterback needed to hear what the coach had to say. To ignore the issue would have spelled certain defeat, and this game was too precious to squander.

We've all seen these sideline conversations on television. Some quarterbacks are focused and listening carefully; some nervously glance back and forth while their coach gives instructions. Others almost seem cavalier, shrugging their shoulders. And when this happens, we see the coach's face become more intense, as if to say, "You listen to me, Buster! This whole game depends on it." We've even seen coaches grab their field commanders by the shoulders to make certain they don't miss anything.

How many weddings have you been to? A dozen? More?

And have you ever watched the groom's face? Does he remind you of the quarterback? Is he glancing left and right, even acting as though it's just another day? Or is he focused, listening to every word being said, as though his future depended on it?

Naturally, most grooms have a subtle first-night twinkle in their eye. That's to be expected. But what they may not know is that this night is the first night in the most important year of their lives.

If they fail to pay careful attention to what goes on over the next twelve months, the cost may be a lifetime of frustration and nonstop misery. But if they learn to do the right things and establish the right habits, the rewards will be measurable—and fantastic!

The goal of this book is, first of all, to get your focused attention. Then I'm going to do my best to convince you that the first year of your marriage *is*, in fact, the most important year in your life.

MAKING THE EARLY INVESTMENT

Jerry set down his newspaper, swiveled his chair toward the window, and leaned back. "I'm a millionaire," he whispered. "A millionaire!" He closed his eyes and let it sink in.

Ten years earlier, one of Jerry's closest friends from graduate school had come with a proposal. Over breakfast, Clark Boyer had told Jerry about his idea for starting a house-call computer service business. "We're going to name it Compu-Calls," Clark told him. "Today the computer business is where the automobile business was forty years ago—lots of hardware out there but not a lot of convenient, reliable service."

Jerry knew that Clark was above average in the intelligence department. But, even more important, Clark wasn't afraid of hard work. And CompuCalls was a solid idea.

"I need ten thousand dollars," Clark announced, just as breakfast arrived.

Jerry sat for a moment, staring at his bacon and eggs. Ten thousand dollars was a lot of money. He and Dianna had just bought their first home, and he still had a few payments left on his car loan. But Clark was his friend, and Jerry had this sense about the proposal. He wasn't a gambler by nature, but Jerry had confidence in Clark.

"As far as I'm concerned, you're on," Jerry said evenly. "Dianna knows you and trusts you. I'll check with her before I give you my final word, but I think she'll be on board, too," he added, a faint smile forming on his face. "I know you're going to make it work."

Over the next ten years Jerry watched Clark pour himself into his work. CompuCalls hired bright young graduates from their town's community college, and the company grew and thrived. Seven years into the business, Clark was given the "Young Entrepreneur of the Year" award, and several large computer sales companies had begun contacting him about a buyout. Clark kept Jerry informed about the offers.

Three years later, Jerry held the newspaper and read the headlines in the business section that made it official: "Boyer sells CompuCalls for Twelve Million."

Jerry's ten thousand dollars had bought him 15 percent of Clark's company, and now, after a decade, the investment was worth well over a million dollars.

Now here's an interesting question: What are the chances

that the company that just bought CompuCalls will realize the same return on their investment that Jerry made?

Slim and none.

Why? One word: *timing*.

Jerry's investment came early in Clark's business plan. Ten years later the dividend opportunities just aren't the same. Ten years earlier, 15 percent of CompuCalls cost Jerry ten thousand dollars. Today it's costing someone $1.8 million, almost 200 times Jerry's investment. The new company will never get those multiples again.

INVEST IN THE FIRST YEAR

This is a book about the first year of marriage—the first year of *your* marriage. Let's pretend that you and I are having breakfast together, and just before you take your first bite of scrambled eggs I tell you about a great investment opportunity. "You've just gotten married. That's great. And if you do the right things now, I can guarantee a great return on your investment."

I've got your undivided attention.

"But if you decide not to make the investment," I add as a postscript, "your chances for a strong and satisfying marriage are going to be greatly reduced. And if your marriage fails, the consequences are going to be tragic—and expensive."

Then, as with any legitimate investment prospectus, I present you with a few convincing endorsements:

1. People with satisfying marriages live longer, enjoy better health, and report a much higher level of satisfaction about life in general.[2]
2. Married men report a deeper satisfaction about life in general than do single men. Forty percent of married couples say they are very happy, compared to 18 percent of those

divorced and 22 percent of those never married or of unmarried couples living together.[3]

3. Despite the myths about the single life, married men enjoy much more frequent sex (almost twice as often) than single men.[4]

4. Even if you are a bottom-line kind of guy who likes to think in dollars and cents, check this out: Recent statistics show that the average married couple in their fifties has a net worth nearly five times that of the average divorced or single person.[5]

5. Divorce dramatically increases the likelihood of early death from strokes, hypertension, respiratory cancer, and intestinal cancer. Astonishingly, being a divorced nonsmoker is only slightly less dangerous than smoking a pack (or more) of cigarettes a day and staying married! (Should divorce summons papers come with the surgeon general's warning, too?)[6]

Research guarantees it: A satisfying marriage can bring you more happiness, more money, less sickness, and better sex. I think we've just redefined a no-brainer.

PAY ME NOW OR PAY ME LATER

It's often assumed that marriages fail because of a lack of investment—time, effort, focus, and intentionality. That's true, but only partially.

Mark and I have talked with countless couples whose marriages are flailing—or failing. Many are more than willing to work at it, and work sacrificially. As a matter of fact, some of the guys we know who struggle in their marriages are investing exponentially *more* energy, anxiety, and money trying to keep their marriages alive than couples with healthy marriages will have to invest *during their entire lifetimes.*

The question must be asked: If these couples are working so hard, why are their marriages failing?

It's exactly what Jerry found out with his successful investment in CompuCalls. It's all about *good timing.* Failed marriages are not the result of the lack of investment but the lateness of that investment.

We've seen it happen over and over. Men have come to us for help only after their marriages are in deep trouble—in some cases, headed perilously toward divorce. A man may become motivated to work on his marriage when it's in critical condition. The work and the sacrifices he makes may be nothing short of heroic. But tragically, they come awfully late.

A DESPERATE SITUATION

He called to say that he had to talk—immediately! "Becky has left me. She won't even talk to me. What am I going to do?"

Bill was desperate. He knew he was about to lose the very thing that mattered to him the most—his family. Over coffee, Bill admitted that he had failed. Through tears he confessed that he had neglected his wife. And now she had moved out.

"I'll do anything," Bill vowed, his jaw set with determination. "I'll do anything to get her back."

Over the next months, Bill began the long, slow climb to rebuild Becky's trust. She was understandably skeptical. The emotional scars were too deep for a quick fix. Bill was beginning to realize that, after taking fifteen years to carelessly dismantle his marriage, it was unlikely that it could be rebuilt in a matter of months.

Can Bill's marriage be saved? Absolutely, particularly if

he's willing to do the costly work he promised to do—work he should have done fifteen years before. But this kind of rebuilding can be exhausting. The challenge is often so demanding, so humbling, and so uncomfortable—and the progress so slow—that many men simply give up.

When Mark and I first talked about writing this book, we brought to mind guys like Bill. There have been times when it felt as though we were trying to stop a man in the middle of a free fall from a high cliff. It's been painful for us, but our discomfort has no comparison to the agony of these men.

I've never met a man who said, "I am choosing to invest poorly"—financially or in marriage. But many men simply do. Their minimal net worth has been the result of neglect. Sheer default.

Making careless investments comes easily; it takes intentional planning to invest wisely.

How Does This Happen?

Given the value of a great marriage, it doesn't make sense that men would scorn making a sound investment early on. However, so many make this mistake. I want to suggest two theories about why this happens:

The Conquest Phenomenon

Some men act as though their work is done the moment their bride says "I do." It's almost as though, on their wedding day, they take their to-do list and put a check mark next to "find a wife." Then, after the honeymoon, it's back to work—and back to that to-do list—with many more battles to win and more check marks to make.

Perhaps the most interesting part of this phenomenon in

men is that, at the same moment they're feeling a sense of finality about their wedding-day accomplishment, their brides are seeing it as just the beginning.

Choosing Not to Choose

This book is based on a single foundational assumption: Your marriage and your life are going to be a hundred times more satisfying, more resilient, and more prosperous if you intentionally develop the right habits in the first year—when the investment is fairly "inexpensive."

If you undervalue this first year and develop bad habits, a solid marriage will be much more expensive to recover later on—or these habits may eventually destroy your marriage.

TIME-TESTED PRINCIPLES

As you and I begin to explore this first-year investment strategy, I want to unveil a treasure that is thousands of years old. Listen to this amazing piece of advice, tucked in the Old Testament between instructions on divorce and directions for the proper use of millstones when making a loan agreement (no kidding):

> If a man has recently married, he must not be sent to war or have any other duty laid on him. For one year he is to be free to stay at home and bring happiness to the wife he has married.
>
> DEUTERONOMY 24:5

Although the prospects of such a thing may sound hilarious or outrageous to you, there are some interesting investment principles buried here that you'll want to take seriously.

The Challenge Principle— "For one year"

Most guys love a contest. We gravitate toward the competitive. Well, here's a huge challenge: If you want to have a great marriage, don't do anything for a whole year except *learn to love your wife.*

I'm pretty sure I know what you're thinking. *C'mon, be reasonable. I've got work to do. If I were to take a whole year off, I'd be fired from my job—and that wouldn't be good for either of us.*

Don't worry. I'm not advocating unemployment. Just intentionality. Your job in your first year of marriage is to become an expert on *one* woman—your wife—and to learn, better than anyone else in the world, how to "bring her happiness." And the Old Testament advice is to take one year, ONE WHOLE YEAR. A weekend seminar or a great book about marriage will not be enough—not even the standard five-session premarital counseling commitment. There's no other way to say it: It's a big investment!

The ADD Principle— "not be sent to war or have any other duty laid on him"

Like folks who suffer from Attention Deficit Disorder (ADD), our problem often is our lack of focus. We're distracted by things our wives don't see—things they may not even care about.

Because you've checked "get married" off your list, you may be tempted to pay more attention to other unfinished things, such as going on to graduate school, landing a good job, or staying in shape physically. But now that you're married, your most important assignment *is* working on building this relationship with your wife.

21

The Reciprocity Principle—"bring happiness to the wife he has married"

Chalk it off to our humanness, but most of us have this backwards. We're eager for our wives to find ways to make *us* happy.

My friend Gary Smalley tells the story of the newlywed couple who moved into the house across the street from Hank and Edna. Soon Edna noticed that when the young groom came home from work each day, instead of pulling into the garage, he parked his car in the driveway and walked down the sidewalk to the front door.

She also noticed that he always had something in his hand—a wrapped gift, a bunch of flowers, or some other special item. He'd ring the doorbell, his wife would answer the door, he'd present the gift, and they'd embrace.

Edna couldn't help herself. One evening after dinner she told Hank all about the couple and what the young husband did each day.

"Why don't you start doing that, Hank?" she whined.

"Well," Hank stammered, "I guess I could." He took a deep breath. "I *could* do that—but I don't even *know* that lady."

Regardless, Edna had it right. It was Hank's job to remember what it was like when he was romancing her.

Early in our marriage my wife, Bobbie, said it to me this way: "I just want to know that, even though you're busy, once in a while you stop and think about me."

Okay, you might be thinking, *but what should my wife do for me?*

That's a fair question, but the answer is sobering. This Old Testament admonition says absolutely nothing about your wife's job. She's given no direction at all. But this is where the reciprocity part comes in. When you make her happiness your priority, your wife finds herself compelled to make *you* happy.

Doing everything you can do during this first year to make your wife happy is not just an unselfish act of martyrdom. Having a contented wife will make an immense difference in your *own* happiness.

The book of Proverbs affirms this idea with a touch of humor—in fact, these exact words appear twice in Proverbs: "Better to live on a corner of the roof than share a house with a quarrelsome wife."[7]

Though it's not always the case, unhappy, nagging, contentious, quarrelsome wives are often married to overly busy, nonresponsive, preoccupied, self-absorbed husbands. And, by trial and error, these wives have learned that the only way to get their husbands' attention is to do something annoying.

Your challenge is to choose to pay more attention to your wife during this first year than you do to your neighbor's new car or to the NCAA Final Four on television. And when you make this investment during the first year, your marriage will be far more satisfying for the rest of your life. It'll be worth millions.

Before you turn the page, decide right now to make the next twelve months the most important year of your life.

2

NEEDS: THE YES SPIRAL

Let the wife make the husband glad to come home, and let him make her sorry to see him leave.

MARTIN LUTHER, SIXTEENTH-CENTURY REFORMER

———◆·••◆·◆·◆———

H i, honey, I'm home."
They're the same words you use each day when you come home, but this time the tone of your voice lets your bride know that it's been a rough one. Quitting your job is all you thought about the whole way home.

As you walk into the house, you're confronted by the aroma of something wonderful. Your wife hears your voice, and she hurries to meet you. Before you can put your computer case down, she wraps her arms around your neck and kisses you. She leans in and whispers something flirtatious about the surprise she has in store for you tonight. She pulls back and takes your computer case. Then she reaches up and loosens your tie.

"I've got just the thing for you," she says, leading you to your favorite chair. Next to the chair sits a frosted glass of your favorite beverage, today's newspaper, and the TV remote.

"You sit here and rest awhile," she says. "I'll get the rest of the dinner on the table."

When this scenario is described to a roomful of couples, it doesn't take long for the men to begin groaning and laughing. "Yeah, right," they say. "Like that would ever happen in my house!" For most husbands, this kind of evening isn't something they'd ever expect. It's nothing they'd even dare to dream about.

But hold on. There *are* men who experience this—not every night, of course, but every once in a while. It's enough to make them shake their heads and wonder how they could have been so fortunate to have been given a wife like this. And "dumb luck" simply isn't the right answer.

No, good things like this don't happen by pure chance. They happen when a couple chooses to cherish each other, finding fulfillment in meeting each other's needs in surprising and extravagant ways.

Now—a question for you: "What would make a woman treat her husband this way?"

You know the answer, don't you? A woman acts this way when her husband has gone first. Her lavishness is in direct response to his willingness to cherish her and to respond to her needs. In a healthy marriage, a husband finds great joy in bringing pleasure to his wife, and a wife delights in demonstrating her love in creative ways.

THE PROVERBS 31 MAN!

From time immemorial, people have challenged women with the description of the perfect wife—more like Wonder

Woman—found in Proverbs 31. But when you take a good look at this ancient poem, there's a man hiding in there.

In fact, to understand the Middle Eastern culture in which this poem was composed, it would have been impossible for a married woman to experience this kind of success *without* a pretty unconventional—and terrific—husband!

Her Husband Has Full Confidence in Her (31:11)

Don't you love the sound of that? The Proverbs 31 man "has full confidence" in his wife. There's plenty of maturity—and balance—in their relationship. He doesn't treat his wife like a child, nor does he treat her like she's his mother. He encourages her specific gifts, and, like a plant living in a greenhouse, she blossoms in that environment.

This is a man who trusts his wife's judgment. He's not threatened by her success or by her busy life. This guy's wife manages her home and runs several businesses. And he gives her freedom to invest, freedom to manage the household, freedom to sell what she produces, and freedom to care for the poor and needy.

Over the years, my wife and I have observed this idea of mutual respect among married couples. We've seen couples where the husband is so domineering that his wife lives with fear that she'll make a mistake and her husband will discover it. She's terrorized by the specter of a bounced check or a dented fender. And we've seen couples where the wife is so independent that her husband has no idea what she's up to. Her friends, her daily activities, and her calendar are in a completely different sphere than his—and he's fine with it.

A Proverbs 31 husband has *full confidence* in his wife, and it's clear that he wouldn't be comfortable in either of the above scenarios.

Her Husband Is Respected at the City Gate, Where He Takes His Seat among the Elders of the Land (31:23)

A few questions to consider:

- Is this man respected among his peers because he has a wife who respects him? or
- Does her admiration raise him to higher levels of success and self-respect?
- Is this man's wife respectful of him because of his impeccable character? or
- Is his integrity tied to her high expectations of him?

The right answer to each of these questions: *Yes.*

Her Husband Praises Her (31:28)

The wife of the Proverbs 31 man immediately gains self-esteem from the sterling reputation of her husband. When she's seen with him in public, she swells with pride. His integrity automatically accrues to her! "[Her husband] praises her" (31:28). Few things are more motivating to a woman than words of sincere admiration coming from her husband. The Proverbs 31 man is liberal with these expressions.

Once again the chicken-and-egg question begs to be asked: "Which comes first—the praise or the success?" And once again, the answer is the same: *Yes.*

Because this woman is married to a man who believes in her and verbally honors her and celebrates her success, she grows in confidence and becomes increasingly competent—which produces more praise from her husband, which in turn enhances her achievements. When you meet this woman, you can tell that she's married to some kind of a great guy!

Getting to Yes

Meeting each other's needs leads to an increasing comfort in conversation, which leads to more frequent opportunities for intimacy, which leads to more satisfaction, which leads to a greater motivation to meet each other's needs—and on and on it goes.

We call this the *Yes Spiral,* and it leads to outdoing each other in showing love. Here's how it works:

> *You:* "Hi, sweetie, I'm home." No response from your wife, only the rattling of pans in the kitchen. "How 'bout a little welcome parade for the king of the castle?" The tone of your voice lets her know that you're just kidding.
>
> *Your Bride:* "I'm sorry. I didn't hear you come in. I was just caught up in getting dinner ready." She comes over and wraps her arms around your waist. Looking up at you, she gives you a big kiss. "Hey, I hate to ask you to do this 'cause I know you just got home, but I'm in the middle of cooking and just realized I'm missing a couple different spices. I really need them for this recipe. Could you run out and get them for me?"
>
> *You:* "Sure. What do I need to get?"
>
> *Your Bride:* "You're the best. Here's the list."
>
> *You:* "Oh, I almost forgot. While I'm out, would you call my parents and ask them when I can stop by their house and pick up that package?"
>
> *Your Bride:* "Of course. I haven't talked to your mom in a couple days anyway."
>
> *You walk over to your wife and give her a hug.*

Your Bride: "I love you so much."

You: "I'll get spices for you anytime."

Your Bride: "Hey, mister, if you hurry back, we can talk about some of my own secret spices." As you leave, she's shaking her head, smiling and saying quietly, "You amaze me."

A silly conversation? Maybe. But did you catch how many times you and your wife said yes to each other in this quick exchange?

1. She said yes to your nonverbal request for a warm greeting.
2. You said yes to her request to make a quick trip to the grocery store.
3. She said yes to your request to call your parents about the package.
4. You said yes by giving her a hug.
5. She said yes to any designs you may have had on being intimate tonight—and you didn't even have to ask.

With each affirmation—in words, actions, or attitudes—the view from your *Yes* ascent widens, and the two of you feel freer together, more willing to serve each other, more willing to creatively meet each other's needs.

But what if you and your wife chose another route:

You: "Hi, sweetie, I'm home." No response from your wife, only the rattling of pans in the kitchen. "How 'bout a little welcome parade for the king of the castle?" The tone of your voice contains just a hint of sarcasm.

Your Bride: "I'm sorry. I didn't hear you come in. I was just caught up in getting dinner ready." She stays in the kitchen and calls out to you from there. "Hey, I hate to ask you to do this 'cause I know you just got home, but I'm in the middle of cooking and just realized I'm missing a couple different spices. I really need them for this recipe. Could you run out and get them for me?"

You (thumbing through the mail): "Why didn't you get them when you were out? You just got groceries yesterday."

Your Bride: "I didn't realize this recipe called for them. I've had a few other things on my mind, you know." Her tone of voice has an edge. "Here's the list."

You: "We'll just have to do without your little spices tonight. I'm not going out again. Not after the day I had. Hey, did you call my parents about when I'm supposed to stop by to pick up the package?"

Your Bride: "You told me *you* were going to do it. I can't do *everything*. I have a job, too, you know."

You: "Fine. I guess we won't pick it up. It doesn't matter to me anyway."

Your Bride: "Excuse me. I need to go to the grocery store. Dinner will be a little late tonight." Her words are barely audible through her clenched teeth as she heads for the door—"You amaze me."

You can feel the tension, can't you? As you and your wife say no to each other's needs, each of you becomes less willing to say yes. The descending *No Spiral* becomes tighter and tighter.

You feel trapped, less willing to give, and not at all interested in meeting each other's needs.

Consider the expenditure of energy in these two conversations. The first is smooth and effortless, though it takes a willingness at times to respond in ways that may feel less convenient. Not only do you love your wife more after this quick exchange, but you actually feel better about yourself. The second conversation — well, it is completely draining, leaving you feeling exhausted.

"OF COURSE I'D DIE FOR HER, BUT . . ."

You may be thinking, *I understand about how conflict is more draining than peacefulness — but what if I don't feel like doing what my wife needs me to do?* So you take a deep breath and ask me the question you really don't want to ask: "Are you suggesting that I suck it up and go to the grocery store anyway, even though my heart's not in it?"

Yes, that's exactly what I'm suggesting.

The biblical mandate is perfectly clear: "Husbands, love your wives, just as Christ loved the church and gave himself up for her."[8] Love is always linked to *action,* even if we don't feel like it. Because you *say* you love your wife, your choice must always be to *do* things that please her, regardless of what may seem to be pure inconvenience.

In the *Yes Spiral* conversation, you demonstrated active love, and the feelings followed close behind. You felt great. But in the *No Spiral* conversation, you did exactly what you believed you had a right to do, exactly what you felt like doing. But by the time your wife stormed out of the house to get the spices, you were both tied up in knots. You were justified in claiming your right to unwind after a rough day, but you felt awful.

Ask a man if he'd be willing to die for his wife, and it's

very likely he'll say that he would. With visions of evil executioners offering the choice between our lives or our brides', we'd courageously give ourselves. "Take me instead," we'd say, with heroism oozing from every pore.

This kind of dying is the easy kind — quick, valiant, offering a clear choice between selfishness and sacrifice. But let's face it — it's highly unlikely that this will ever happen to us. "Laying down our lives" gets demonstrated in smaller and less visible or applaudable ways. You are charged with considering your wife's needs above your own. In this sense her request is more important than the fatigue you're feeling from a big day and your need to put your feet up. A *lot* more important!

"But what if meeting my wife's needs like this doesn't come naturally," you may argue. "Responding well to my wife's surprise requests is something I'm lousy at." Or how about this one? "My wife knows I don't do housework." Or this? "I'm just naturally a competitor, so showing consideration to other drivers on the highway just isn't who I am, even when my wife pleads with me to calm down."

Okay, so these things don't come naturally. Did learning to ride a bicycle come naturally, or did you have to work at it? How about swimming? Or learning to read? Or using a computer? Did these things come naturally, or did you *learn* them? And what did it take for these to become skills? That's easy to answer. You *wanted* to master them — and so you did.

What Does She Need?

Late one evening a couple went for a walk around the neighborhood. They walked past two boys who were down on their knees under a streetlight. They were searching through the grass for something. Carefully they swept their hands back and forth.

"What's the matter?" the man said to the kids. "You boys lose something?"

"Yeah," one of the kids responded without looking up. "My friend lost his pocketknife."

"Did he lose it here?" the woman asked.

"No," said the boy, looking up at the woman. "He lost it down the street, but the light's a lot better here."

A silly joke, but it contains a powerful message: we do sometimes try to meet our wives' needs based on what might be convenient for us. But we're far away from finding what our wives are looking for. This may keep us busy, but it's not going to help us find the "lost pocketknife" that matters most to our wives.

So here's an idea. In order of importance, jot down five or six things you think your wife most wants from you. Be as general or as specific as you like. Then tell your wife what you're working on, and ask her to make her own list—without seeing yours. Then schedule an appointment with her to compare your lists. You may want to begin the conversation by telling her about the boys looking for the lost pocketknife in the wrong place. This will help her understand what you're up to.

Once you have her list, start doing the first thing she asks for, and let the fun begin.

What Do I Need?

Jeremy walked into Mark's office and plopped down on the overstuffed chair in the corner. Mark looked up from his work. Jeremy was clearly irritated.

"After a bad day," Jeremy began, "I need my wife to be there for me. But I have the hardest time putting anything in words. I want to tell Cindy what I need, but it's like my 'asker' is broken—so I pick a fight instead."

"Hey, thanks for being there for me," Jeremy would say sarcastically to Cindy, frustrated because she couldn't read his mind.

The evening was destined to be miserable for both Jeremy and Cindy.

"I've had enough of these tense evenings at home," Jeremy admitted. "What can I do?"

Okay, let me ask you: What would *you* say to Jeremy? How would you help him solve this problem?

We know that Cindy really *does* love Jeremy. But, on the days he needs her most, he doesn't give her much to work with, does he?

First of all, this couple needs a clean slate. And that can come only when Jeremy is courageous enough to admit that his sarcasm and fight-picking strategies are childish and not helpful. Next, Cindy needs a target—a clear picture of what her husband needs from her. Jeremy may simply want to reverse the exercise I suggested in the last section, only this time, the two of them list the things that Jeremy needs.

You may also want to take a look at the companion book, *What Every Bride Needs to Know*—at the list of an expert's opinion of what most men need most from their wives (see page 33). It may take some gut-level honesty to admit that you *need* your wife, and then a little more work to be honest about what your own needs are.

But if you want to actually find that pocketknife, you'll need to move to places where the search may not be as easy.

3

SPIRITUAL UNITY: KEEPING YOUR HEAD IN THE ONLY GAME THAT MATTERS

Marriage for the Christian is a continuous sacrament, an act of praise and obedience, and a means of grace that is inherently every bit as "spiritual" as anything that goes on in a monastery, or in any church or mission field for that matter, and every bit as important (or more so) than any other "work" that one might do in the world.

MIKE MASON, *THE MYSTERY OF MARRIAGE*

❧

Bobbie and I had been married for less than a year. She was trying to finish college and was holding a part-time job as a dental assistant. I was in youth work, making less than minimum wage. Early one afternoon we paid a visit to Bobbie's doctor and discovered that she—we, really—was pregnant.

I was excited about the baby, but the timing was a bit different from my original plan. Not only were we not in any kind of financial condition to add another person to our family, but I was still trying to figure out who *I* was and how I was going to be a good husband. I was also trying to figure out who this woman was, and now I was headed for fatherhood. "Overwhelmed?"—nice try, but it doesn't come close.

We drove home from the doctor's office with virtually no words exchanged. By the time I had unlocked our apartment door, emotion had completely swept over me. Tears were streaming down my face. We walked into the kitchen, and Bobbie pulled out a chair and sat down. I collapsed on the floor in front of her and buried my face in her knees. This was not normal behavior for me. Sobs came from somewhere I had never visited before. Bobbie just sat there, probably wondering who this man was and why he was crying so inconsolably.

After a few minutes, I was able to speak. "I can't do this," was all I could say. "I can't do this."

Strange as it may sound to you, it was then that becoming a good husband and a good dad became achievable goals. Why? Because at that very moment, filled with sheer panic, I turned to *God* for help.

Getting Naked

Taking the initiative with regard to spiritual things in your marriage is not easy. It's going to take some honest effort. This is especially true if you can't remember ever seeing your parents express any sort of spiritual intimacy together.

For example, for many men there is the horror of an embarrassing "soul nakedness" that comes when they're called on to pray in public, much less one-on-one with their wives. Maybe you've seen an otherwise fearless man reduced to a quivering puddle of warm Jell-O simply by hearing the words, "Okay, Big John, why don't you close this meeting with prayer."

In many ways, you can judge the quality of a couple's intimacy by looking at the comfort level of their conversation in two areas: sex and spiritual things. Conversation about physical intimacy forces you to reveal hidden parts of your mind and your body; conversation about spiritual intimacy uncovers your soul.

Before going any further, let me tell you what I'm *not* talking about here. Spiritual intimacy is not about theological precision or agreeing to the same set of religious doctrines. It's not that these things don't matter. Surely they do. It's just that mere mutual assent to a set of ideas *about* God doesn't go far enough, either in your relationship with Jesus or in your relationship with your wife.

Both relationships require an additional step: an openhearted willingness to unveil the secret places, to explore each other's hearts with curiosity and pleasure, to disclose spiritual doubts and fears, and to celebrate new levels of understanding—and to do these things in the context of ordinary living.

"How 'bout that huge hawk up there," I may say to Bobbie as we're driving along the highway near our home. "Isn't God amazing?"

"Come, look at this rainbow," I've heard her call from the porch. These things thrill our eyes and lift our hearts.

We love music, especially old hymns and classical music. We also love jazz and some contemporary Christian music. In the car we'll sometimes stop talking and turn up a favorite, much-loved CD. I mean, *way* up. This music takes our spirits to another plane, and we go there together. Similarly, we rarely miss church, not because we feel guilty if we don't go but because we know that this experience of worship takes us into the presence of the living God. And when we've been with him, everything looks different.

We have a retired friend. Not long ago he and his wife attended a marriage retreat. Even though they had passed their golden wedding anniversary a long time before, our friend and his wife were looking for ways to improve their marriage. The gentleman told us that he took pride in his depth of understanding of his wife and in building a successful marriage. (In fact, because they had done so well, this veteran couple had been asked to speak at several marriage retreats themselves.) But this weekend, as a participant, our friend saw something about his wife that he had never seen before.

On the retreat, one of the exercises required the wife to write down the most meaningful ways her husband showed love to her—and for him to do the same for her. With a disarming smile, our friend explained that, after decades of marriage, he expected no surprises from his wife's list. When his wife handed him her list, however, the first item *did* surprise him. He had expected her to say something about how much she appreciated his unsolicited help in cleaning the house, or perhaps how much she enjoyed their weekly date night. But number one on her list of the "most meaningful things my husband does to show me love" was this: when you pray with me and take the initiative about our spiritual life.

Our friend had always considered the carrying out of spiritual practices in his home to be a matter of duty. It had never occurred to him that these things were also a powerful way of *expressing love to his wife*. In her mind, it was number one.

But How?

You may have no trouble agreeing that these things are important, even *very* important. You know that your wife wants to know your heart, not just your mind and your body. You know that, as you explore spiritual things and place yourselves in God's presence together, good things will happen. But you're asking, "How do I *do* that?"

You may be encouraged to know that when a large number of Christian leaders were asked what they do in their own marriages to cultivate spiritual intimacy, their answers were completely unique. Almost every couple did something a little different.[9]

When Mark meets with couples before their weddings, he suggests the K.I.S.S. (keep it simple, stupid) approach to establishing a pattern for spiritual intimacy in marriage. He makes the simple suggestion that couples start with at least one regular habit: praying before meals, praying together at bedtime, attending church and Sunday school, or reading a devotional book together. Mark asks the groom and his bride to come up with some visible practice that will regularly remind them that theirs is a Christian marriage.

Look at the way the Old Testament describes spiritual intimacy: "Love the LORD your God with all your heart and with all your soul and with all your strength. . . . Talk about [these commandments] when you sit at home and when you walk along the road, when you lie down and when you get up.[10]

Love the LORD your God: Your proposal to the woman who is now your bride began with a learning and a longing and eventually progressed to a *decision* — "Will you marry me?" In the same way, your relationship with God begins with an understanding of who he is and the experience of a deep sense of lostness without him, and then progresses to a decision: "I want to follow you."

Talk about them when you sit at home: I've already mentioned our experiences of spotting a soaring hawk or a spectacular rainbow from the deck. Seeing these things and commenting, "Isn't God amazing?" reminds us that, by his voice alone, God created each of these wonderful things. There's no need to add anything to make it more "spiritual." There's no need to say, "You know, it's just like Rev. Jones said at the morning service."

Over the years, at special times or because of unusual situations we were facing, Bobbie and I have found time to pray out loud together before we go to sleep. There's nothing fancy about these prayers. They're simply a chance for the two of us to speak to our heavenly Father as though he's right there in the bedroom with us. Truth be told, he *is!*

Hinge Points and Prayer Hooks

Because they represent "corners" in their day, Mark and Susan refer to sitting down, getting up, or going to bed as "hinge points," the most natural arenas for making a spiritual connection. Susan may walk past Mark as they're crawling out of bed early in the morning, kiss him on the cheek, and say, "God is good." At night, Mark may reach across the bed and take Susan's hand before they fall asleep. "You want to pray tonight?" Mealtimes can be another hinge point for you and your wife. Pausing, holding hands, and saying a blessing is a natural hinge point.

There's no fanfare, no great preparation or training for this. But it *does* connect predictable moments in our walk with God, turning ordinary everyday things into spiritual things.

Bobbie and I have a similar thing we call "prayer hooks." These are familiar places, things, or situations we have intentionally connected to prayer. For example, when we're driving to church on Interstate 4 and begin slowing down for the Anderson Street exit, that's a prayer hook. So we pray (we keep going, with our eyes open) for the Sunday morning worship service and for Sunday school. We ask God to speak to us during this time in his house.

The first thing in the morning, when I turn on the lights in my office and see the green chair in the corner, that's a prayer hook. It's as though the chair is speaking to me and inviting me to kneel down and pray.

Some of my other prayer hooks are connected to some pretty mundane things, but they work. For example, when I use my ChapStick, I pray for my son-in-law Christopher, because he's a serious ChapStick user, too. When I take out the trash, I pray for my son-in-law Jon. He taught me to keep extra bags in the bottom of the trash container, so when I see the empty bags down there, I remember to pray for him. One time my friend Jake gave me one of those great trivia facts. He told me that monkeys peel bananas from the bottom because they're easier to open that way. So guess who I pray for every time I peel a banana from the bottom? There are more, but you get the idea.

These are the kinds of things the author of the Old Testament book of Deuteronomy had in mind. Spiritual intimacy with God simply means to include him in your day—especially in the little things.

BECOMING A FAITHFUL BRIDE

As you begin your life as a married man, it's interesting to note that one of the word pictures God uses in the Bible to describe your relationship with him is precisely what you've just experienced—marriage. But in this case *he's* the groom and *you're* his bride!

> As a bridegroom rejoices over his bride,
>   so will your God rejoice over you.
>
> ISAIAH 62:5

Mother Teresa understood this. She had just finished teaching about God's standards for families when a man stood up and challenged her. "With all due respect, Mother Teresa," he said, "how can you—someone who has never been married—tell us about what kind of husbands and wives we're supposed to be?"

Unruffled by the man's abruptness, the tiny nun from Calcutta spoke—with a twinkle in her eye. "Sir, that's where you're wrong," she said. "I *am* married. And sometimes Jesus is very hard to live with!"

The man quietly sat down.

The question is clear: What can you learn from God's relationship with you, from the perfect Groom, about what it means to walk with your wife as *her* faithful groom? Here are some examples:

God Is Attentive

Can you imagine what it would be like to be married to someone who never stopped listening to you? Night or day, at a moment's notice—his ears are tuned to your every request. God is in constant communication with you. Sometimes this "communication" is without words. He's on call, just by his presence. Occasionally he "speaks" to you through circumstances, through books, or through the voices of people. And, of course, he speaks clearly when we read the Bible. God's attentiveness is his full-time activity. Doesn't that sound great? Can you imagine how content your bride would be if she had a groom like that?

God Is Accountable

One of the great mysteries about God is that he is really *three* persons—Father, Son, and Holy Spirit. And these three operate in perfect sync. Nothing is done without each one's oversight and permission. With this Groom, there's perfect accountability.[11]

Even though Bobbie and I have lived in a number of cities throughout our marriage, I've done my best to be part of a group of Christian men—friends—with whom I can study, pray, and be honest about my defeats and victories. Mark has done the same. In fact, some groups get specific about keeping each other accountable in their marriages. In one such group, all the husbands made a pledge to follow this training plan. See what you think:

- I will pray for my wife at least once every day.
- I will pray with my wife at least once a week.
- I will do something every day to grow in my faith.
- I will agree to answer any question from anyone in this group and to give a full and honest answer. "I'd rather not talk about that right now" is not an acceptable response.
- If at any point this entire group agrees that I need to change a behavior they believe could be destructive to my marriage, my family, or my integrity, I agree to do everything in my power to make the change immediately.
- I will respond to my wife's expressed needs with a wholehearted, unqualified yes in my words, attitudes, and actions.

As you can tell, these guys are serious. Now, I have a question for you: Would your wife like to be the bride of a man like this?

God Is Humble

God visited the planet Earth in Jesus Christ. If ever there was anyone who had good reasons to strut, it was Jesus.

Everything that was created — billions of galaxies, the nucleus of a carbon atom, a tree frog — came into existence at the mere sound of his voice. And with that same voice he holds all things together. But he refused to forcibly use his power. Instead, he laid it aside and took "the very nature of a servant."[12] He chose the way of humility.

Arrogance is a strange disease. It makes everyone sick except the person who has it. I'm sure *you* don't have any interest in being married to someone like this. Neither does your bride. She'd probably rather be married to a man who tenderly served her than to a self-absorbed, swaggering fool. Probably.

God Has Integrity

How many lies does it take to make a man a liar? How many acts of unfaithfulness does it take to make a man a philanderer? How many things does a man need to steal before he is considered a thief? The answer to each of these questions is the same: *only one*. This is a cruel thing, but it's the truth.

The faithful groom has figured out how to take his passions, his character, his mind, and his activities and blend them into consistency. No single area of his life lags behind. A hidden camera would reveal no surprises. God *is* this kind of Groom, and we *know* how it feels to be the "bride" of such a Man.

GET IN THE GAME — SUCK IT UP AND GET IT DONE

Taylor and Laurie were thinking about getting married, but they didn't think they were ready. They wanted to see if they could build some spiritual unity first. They set out to do this by praying together and having a thirty-minute devotional time each week. After a few weeks, Taylor was about to scrap the whole idea. It just wasn't working. In his eagerness to do *something*, Taylor was taking a Bible story and expounding on it like a mini-sermon. Laurie wanted to have a good attitude, but she felt more like a third grader in Sunday school.

When Laurie confessed to Taylor how she felt about his "lectures," he could have thrown in the towel. But Taylor wasn't a quitter. And he did what you and I hate to do. He stopped and asked for directions from someone he trusted. And then he tried again, this time remembering the K.I.S.S. principle.

Taylor trimmed his thirty-minute lesson to five minutes of reading verses from a psalm and then talking *with* Laurie about what it was saying to them. Occasionally, he would read from a devotional book, and again they'd discuss it together. Now, instead of Laurie feeling as though her fiancé had become an overnight clergyman, she discovered in Taylor a soul mate. A *spiritual* friend.

God never designed our marriages to be held together simply by sharing a street address or sex or sports or activities or even common beliefs. There is so much more to it than this. The often elusive quality of spiritual intimacy gives you and your bride a whole person-to-person union. It links you together with God and opens up a brand-new dimension to your marriage. Like hitting the "Surround Sound" button on your stereo, spiritual intimacy makes your marriage more magnificent than you could ever imagine.

It's exactly what you and your bride are looking for.

4

FAMILY OF ORIGIN: A RIVER RUNS THROUGH IT

We say, "the two shall become one." That's fine, but the trouble is that six people marry and sometimes things get a little crowded around the house. There are two sets of parents and two children of the past.

DAVID SEAMANDS, *PUTTING AWAY CHILDISH THINGS*

———◆━◆◆◆━◆———

I t was the longest, no-sleep trip I had ever taken. In 1973, fifteen high school boys and four leaders (I was one of them) borrowed a Winnebago and a pickup truck and drove nonstop from Chicago, Illinois, to Denver, Colorado. Then we boarded a school bus and drove nonstop to Ouray, Utah, where we put in for a white-water ride down the Green River.[13] The road trip from front to back—I drove most of it—took twenty-six hours, and we were all completely exhausted.

Just before we climbed aboard the largest rubber rafts any of us had ever seen, the guide talked us through the dangers of the trip we were about to take. "Inattentive" wouldn't come close to describing his listeners, who were yawning and slouching from road fatigue. He told us about the power of the current on top of the river and down below. He told us that there *would* be times when some of us would go for "unintentional swims." And he told us what to do and what not to do when it happened.

"Keep your legs up," he said. "If you drive them down, your feet can get caught under a rock, and you could be killed." His bluntness lifted some sleepy eyelids. Then he said something like this: "The river looks dangerous enough. But the danger you can see doesn't compare to what's happening below—just beneath the surface."

Over the next four days, the admonitions of the guide proved true. Many of us became "unintentional swimmers." Some of the biggest boys—football players and wrestlers—who thought the guide was exaggerating about the power of the currents below discovered that his warnings were completely true.

The most memorable moment occurred late one afternoon as our raft went straight into a frothing, raging "hole." In an instant, Bill Jackson, perhaps the most athletic boy on the trip, went airborne like a guided missile—from the front of the raft all the way to about fifteen feet behind us, landing with a huge splash. During the next few minutes of watery violence, we grabbed the ropes and hunkered down, hoping to avoid the same fate. Jax kept his legs up and rode it out with us, looking more like a cork than a boy. By nightfall we were able to joke about it, but when it was happening, there was nothing to laugh about.

Thankfully, we all made it to the end of the line safely. Some of us had cuts and bruises as trophies, but we made it nonetheless.

MARRIAGE CURRENTS

Marriage is like a white-water run in a river raft. We ride along, experiencing new adventures at every turn. But the things we bring to our marriage from the family in which we grew up are like the powerful currents beneath. There are times when we enjoy the currents above that shoot us along the river. But there are also times when the currents below become destructive danger zones—especially if they sneak up on us and surprise us.

When Bobbie and I were first married, our lives were filled with unexpected things about the way her family did things compared to mine. One night, after we had finished dinner, Bobbie offered to get me a bowl of ice cream.

"Sure," I said, "that would be great."

In a few minutes, she set a bowl of ice cream in front of me. I mean she brought me a BOWL of ice cream. "This would feed a family of six," I said, not realizing how thoughtless and condescending it sounded.

Bobbie wasn't amused.

I had grown up in a home where frugality and restraint were sacramental. Even though we were fourth-generation American Germans, that sober-minded, desks-in-straight-rows, no-running-in-the-hallways structure was tattooed to our chromosomes. When my mother put ice cream in front of us, it was a small single scoop. If we had been perfect children and Dad was out of town, maybe a scoop and a half. Bobbie's family, on the other hand, knew nothing of such culinary restraint. So to Bobbie, a BOWL of ice cream was perfectly normal.

And there's the most important word in this chapter: *Normal.*

What was *normal* for Bobbie was *not* a scoop. A bowl of

ice cream was a BOWL of ice cream. That was normal. My *normal* was something else. And I brought plenty of my own undercurrents to our marriage.

My dad didn't pay much attention to the neighbors. He wasn't rude or unkind to them. It's just that he didn't go out of his way to speak with them or get to know them. Participating in neighborhood parties would have ranked just below gargling with gasoline on his list of enjoyable activities. To me, *normal* was my dad, committed to spending time with his own family but coming and going with a wave and a hello to the neighbors — nothing more than that.

The first time I visited Bobbie's home in Virginia, she was in the kitchen, putting the finishing touches on a beautiful birthday cake. Although it was fairly early in our relationship, we were definitely boyfriend and girlfriend — an item, so to speak.

"Who's that for?" I asked.

"General Illig," she replied with delight.

"Who's General Illig?" I asked, trying not to sound jealous.

"He's our next-door neighbor," she answered.

I remember being completely shocked. *I'm sure he's a nice guy, but why would you waste a perfectly good cake on a neighbor?*

To me, *normal* would have been not even knowing *when* the neighbor's birthday was. What's more, *normal* wouldn't have included buying a birthday card if I *had* known. And it certainly wouldn't have included making a birthday cake — from scratch, no less! What was normal to Bobbie looked like a complete waste of time and energy to me. A good neighbor is a guy who isn't a bother, who keeps his house painted, his lawn mowed, and his weeds to a minimum. Period.

Now, here's something very important about this "normal" issue. Most of the *normals* that you and I bring to our marriages are amoral—neither good nor bad, neither right nor wrong. They're simply the things we were accustomed to as we were growing up—the things we didn't question because it was all we knew. It's a safe bet that most of your *normals* are different from your bride's *normals*.

Someone has suggested that everyone enters marriage with his or her own "ten commandments" about what's normal. But the only time these commandments are identified is when the spouse breaks one of them. Until then, they are only subconscious.

Both of our daughters and their fiancés did their premarital work with Mark and Susan. And Julie and Missy have both told us that, without question, the most productive (and most unsettling) premarital exercise they did centered around this topic of *normal*.

By making use of a genogram—a special family-tree diagram that begins with the grandparents—Mark and Susan are able to sift through the information to discover patterns of *normal*. They ask such questions as, "What would a child growing up in this system have learned about what a normal husband looks like? A normal wife? What does a normal marriage look like? Normal conflict? Normal spiritual life?"

Making Your Own Genogram

To do your own genogram, you and your bride can start by each drawing a family tree that looks something like this:

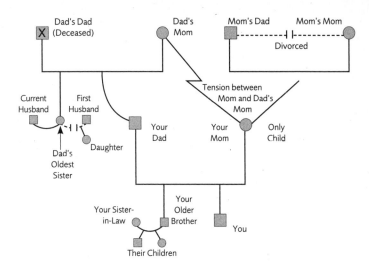

When Mark and Susan complete their work on the genogram with a couple, they ask the bride or groom to give them a brief description of each person in his or her own genogram. These descriptions can vary widely from very specific comments— "president of IBM," "lifetime homemaker," or "serving time"—to more general words such as "nurturer," "strict," or "a jerk." As couples share this information, Mark urges them to say the first things that come to their minds, not to think too long about their answers. Their honest and immediate responses will always provide the best clues to each one's sense of *normal*.

Once these initial descriptive notes are obtained, Mark asks for more information about parents and grandparents—always asking three questions:

- What can you tell us about their marriage?
- What can you tell us about how they dealt with conflict?
- What can you tell us about their spiritual life?

Mark and Susan also ask the bride and groom if there are any models of great marriages in their family systems. Then they ask about any tension between people within each of their families. From this information, Mark writes a "Normal Report," which gives the bride and groom a picture of what a typical person growing up in his or her family would see as normal. This report answers five questions:

1. What would someone growing up in this family system see as a normal husband?
2. What would someone growing up in this family system see as a normal wife?
3. What would someone growing up in this family system see as a normal marriage?
4. What would someone growing up in this family system see as a normal way to deal with conflict?
5. What would someone growing up in this family system see as a normal spiritual life for a married couple?

As Mark and Susan talk couples through the answers to these questions, the response is amazing. The vast majority of couples really get it. They leave this session with their eyes wide open, seeing their need to enter marriage prepared to do more than "what comes naturally."

Note this, too: Though there's much to be gained by working through a genogram with trained counselors, you can make some fascinating discoveries identifying your *normals* using the same process on your own.

SAMPLE "TEN COMMANDMENTS" OF *NORMAL*

After you construct your genogram, it might be helpful to make up a pretend list of "ten commandments." To get you started, here's a list of "commandments" that we've observed. How many would you identify as normal for you?

1. Married women only work until babies are born. Then they stay at home.
2. The fun of Christmas morning is sleeping late.
3. Sex is never to be discussed.
4. The fun of Christmas morning is waking up early and getting completely dressed for a big family breakfast.
5. Two people who really love each other should never argue.
6. No home is complete without a cat.
7. There's no room for childish silliness.
8. Men always do the driving.
9. Two people who really love each other have plenty of arguments.
10. Husbands always plan the vacations.
11. Two children—max.
12. Being late is cute.
13. Men do not need to engage in deep conversation. It's not natural.
14. Being on time is critical.
15. Men always initiate sex.
16. Women whose husbands don't engage in deep conversation are free to tell their friends about it.
17. Life is fun.
18. How many children a couple has is up to God.
19. Kitchen cabinet doors are a nuisance, which is why they should be left open.
20. Women hide their purchases from their husbands.
21. Men don't do housework.

22. Alcohol, in any form, is a bad idea.
23. Except for anger, men do not show their emotions.
24. The house should always be immaculate.
25. Cars are to be idolized and should never be dirty.
26. Dinner isn't dinner without a glass of wine. Football isn't football without a beer.
27. Cars are transportation. Period.
28. Saying a prayer before a meal is a nonnegotiable. Even at McDonald's.
29. Husbands write the checks.
30. Men should volunteer to do housework without being asked.
31. A man should always hold the door for his wife.
32. Sandwiches are always made with white bread.
33. Wives do the books.
34. It's not necessary to say a blessing before every meal. God knows we're thankful.
35. Sitting quietly and reading a book is a complete waste of time.
36. A woman should never make more money than her husband.
37. No home is complete without a dog—a really big dog.
38. A hot breakfast will only be possible if you put a lighted match to your cornflakes.
39. A loving husband should be blind to his wife's weight gain. Anything else is conditional love.
40. Watching sports on television is a complete waste of time.
41. Wives are responsible for the warmth and tenderness in the relationship.

42. In-laws are never to be consulted.
43. A basketball goal in the driveway is standard equipment for every house.
44. Screaming is always a bad idea. We never raise our voices. We never yell.
45. Women should be willing to move to follow their husbands' careers.
46. Men do yard work.
47. Couples should never borrow money from their parents.
48. Holding the door for a woman is chauvinistic.
49. Gaining weight is a sure sign that you no longer care about your spouse.
50. You're married for life, so you never need to talk about it.

You may want to take out a piece of paper and write down some of your *normals* that didn't make it onto this list. And go ahead—jot down some of your wife's *normals,* too.

OWNING YOUR UNSPOKEN RULES

The more you're aware of these unspoken rules—your own *normals*—the more you can own them. Instead of putting moral values on them and shaming your wife if she doesn't abide by them as well, you can simply recognize them as what you're familiar with because you learned it as you were growing up.

Often when counselors confront clients about their patterns of *normal,* they're met with skepticism. "That may have been a *normal* in my family," counselees argue, "but it certainly doesn't affect me." Yet, if truth be told, it does. Consider these sobering—even frightening—facts about these patterns:

The Patterns Often Don't Show Up Until a Husband and Wife Begin to Establish Their Own System

Because these hidden rules about what's normal are often invisible to the person who holds them, they often don't reveal themselves before a couple gets married and begins to establish their own home.

During my engagement I owned a car that had a slight steering-wheel pull to the right. And because the available strength in my right arm was greater than the strength in my wallet, I chose to live with it. After a while, I no longer noticed it. When we got married, Bobbie used my car one time because hers was in the shop. "Your car nearly put me in the ditch," she exclaimed when she got back to our apartment. "I could have been killed!" (As I recall, I told her that I had forgotten about it—which until that moment was true—and made some quip about her overreacting.)

Normal was my car pulling to the right, and until Bobbie's *normal* of driving a perfectly safe car encountered mine, I hadn't thought twice about my *normal*.

These Patterns Show Up Most When We Are Experiencing Stress

For many couples, their marriage produces emotional anxiety soon after the honeymoon is over. Loneliness, depression, and frustration over a surprising lack of communication can sneak up on a bride or groom long before all the wedding thank-you notes are written. Because of this stress, you or your wife may drop your guard and expose your *normals* in no time at all.

One evening I was on a church bus filled with kids. We were headed for an outing—bowling, miniature golf, something like that. The driver slammed on the brakes to avoid a car that had illegally sped through an intersection. A teenage boy named Bubba (I'm not kidding), who was standing in the aisle, was caught off guard and found himself sprawled out on the floor. On his way down he let out an expletive at a smoke-alarm decibel. The bus went immediately silent. Bubba looked up. "I don't know where *that* came from," he said sheepishly.

Like you and me, Bubba had patterns of *normal* he could maintain under controlled circumstances and different patterns he expressed while under stress. He may not have known "where that came from," but you and I have a good idea.

Reading Your Genogram Is Like Reading Your X Ray—It's the Truth

When Mark interprets genograms for couples in counseling, he often says, "I'm just reading your X ray." And just like an X ray, the genogram may show a problem that has no visible symptoms.

One of my closest friends recently went in for his annual physical. One of his blood enzymes indicated the possibility of cancer. Further tests confirmed a diagnosis of leukemia. When he told me the story, I asked if he had experienced any symptoms, any pain, any discomfort at all.

"None," he said. "Nothing at all."

But my friend believed the report, and he's in the process of a rigorous procedure to treat it. Not having symptoms can be misleading.

Sometimes We Identify Patterns by Reacting against Them

We are not destined to repeat the *normal* of our family system—but it is possible to wear ourselves out trying to be as *unlike* the inherited pattern as we can.

Mark has told me that, in his family, men tend toward intensity and seriousness. As he became aware of that *normal,* he determined that he would be different. He would be happy, *no matter what!* He spent many of his early years pushing himself to be happy, trying to make everyone around him happy as well. Thinking that he was declaring his independence from his family system, Mark came to find out that he was still being controlled by it.

Couples Seldom Fight About What They Are Fighting About

You may think that you and your bride are having a conflict about money or sex or in-laws or schedules or any one of a number of hot topics. But almost all conflicts in marriage — especially those that become destructive — come from something other than the issue that started them. More often than not, these fights come from a clash of your *normal* — and hers.

The value of beginning the work of defining the *normals* of your own family system early in your marriage is that by knowing them you'll be able to prevent sparks from igniting into an explosion. To avoid a disaster, here's something to consider saying: "You know what? The reason I said that to you was because, when I grew up, this wasn't our *normal.* What you did wasn't bad; it's only that it was unfamiliar to me."

Can you imagine what this could do to quell the battle about to begin?

Cautious Is Better Than Casual

The secret to interpreting your genogram is to focus on potential trouble spots — on places where the undercurrents are moving in conflicting and potentially destructive directions. A smart river guide before a white-water trip isn't going to spend a lot of time talking about the smooth water downstream. He or she will focus on the danger zones.

The purpose of identifying these patterns of *normal* in your marriage is to prepare yourself for the places where you will face the greatest challenges. Actually, being prepared can turn danger into adventure.

What you need to hear is, "This *might* happen" or, "This *could* be a problem you'll have to deal with." In many cases, the potential problem area will not become a problem at all—and the couple will be pleasantly surprised. It's better to be cautious than casual. A stern warning about danger that never materializes is far better than nonchalantly discussing how wonderful the smooth water will be—and far better than being overwhelmed by the rapids.

WORKING ON, NOT JUST IN

When I started my own business in 1986, my business partner and I became acquainted with a book titled *The E-Myth*, written by Michael Gerber. The book gave some great advice—the most helpful of which was never to just work *in* our business. He urged readers not to let the pressures of marketing their product and making payroll distract them from time spent working *on* their business.

This meant that my partner, Mike Hyatt, and I needed to sit down every once in a while and ask the tough questions about where the business was going. It wasn't enough to have a "productive week" or even a "successful month." We had to make sure that our decisions and our activities were moving us in a direction consistent with our vision. We forced ourselves to stop and talk *about* our business, not just get caught up in the work from day to day.

Sometimes these conversations started disagreements between Mike and me about such things as hiring a person to fill a spot—or continuing to do double-duty ourselves. "Couldn't you have just left well enough alone?" someone may have asked. "You know, let sleeping dogs lie?"

You and I are faced with identical situations in our marriages. There are plenty of day-to-day activities to accomplish, plenty to keep us busy. But are we doing the hard work of working *on* our marriages and not just living *in* them?

Mark and I have met thousands of couples. Most of these couples will make it all the way down the river. Many will actually enjoy the ride. But you and your bride don't just want to finish; you want to flourish. You want yours to be an outstanding marriage. The difference between the good ones and the great ones is this fact alone: Everyone works *in* a marriage, but only a few work *on* their marriages. Yours can be one of the great ones.

Enjoy the ride.

5

ROLES: WHEN YOU'RE TRYING TO DECIDE WHO WILL BE ON TOP

> *No marriage can succeed unless it is perme-*
> *ated, saturated, with this spirit of acquiescence,*
> *of continual giving in, of gracious and willing*
> *compliance.*
>
> MIKE MASON, *THE MYSTERY OF MARRIAGE*

———◆·×·◆———

I have always been drawn to team sports. Every man has his own assignment, and if he executes well, the team's chances for success skyrocket. There are few opportunities for the middle linebacker to carry the ball or for the quarterback to intercept a pass. These guys have the responsibilities of their specific positions, and so that's what they do. The same is true in hockey, basketball, soccer, and baseball.

Marriage is *not* a team sport. Your assignment today may be your wife's assignment tomorrow. Her task tomorrow may be yours the next day. Given the *normal* you grew up with—your parents' and grandparents' roles may have been quite fixed—this may be a huge adjustment for you.

Fifty years ago, when a man came home from work, he sat down and waited for the little lady to fix dinner. Now, when you get home and there's no dinner cooking in the oven (your wife may still be at work), you go to the freezer, the refrigerator, or, if you're really cool, the recipe book, and you whip something up for the two of you.

You no longer hustle past a pile of laundry, hoping that someday it'll magically disappear. No, you separate the whites from the darks, and toss a load into the washing machine, along with a dash of detergent.

Your marriage is not football or hockey or basketball or soccer. Your marriage is more like a two-person sailing expedition. Your goal is to get from here to there, and whatever jobs need to get done will get done by whomever happens to have the time to do them. There's no "hey, bailing water isn't my job—I man the rudder." Can you imagine?

THREE ROLES EVERY WIFE NEEDS HER HUSBAND TO PLAY

The roles you play in your marriage are far more important—more strategic—than going down two checklists: roles you take and roles your wife takes. And your roles are not just about what you do around the house. It's clearly about *who* you are.

You Are a Leader

Your chest may have swelled when you read these words: "You are a leader." *A leader?* you might think to yourself. *Now you're talking. It's about time I get the role I deserve around here.*

The leadership I'm talking about isn't the kind of leadership you may be accustomed to seeing. This leadership is a different sort altogether. Why? Because games of intimidation, power, control, and manipulation are utterly ineffective in marriage. A leader who demands that he be taken seriously simply on the basis of his position of leadership is a miserable leader.

Your first exposure to a man assuming leadership in marriage was your own dad. If he was a perfect example, you're blessed. All you have to do now is follow in his footsteps. If not, you're going to have to look elsewhere for a model.

Your parents' generation gave them husband prototypes like Ward Cleaver, whose voice, when he spoke to June, never reached a decibel higher than the sound of a marshmallow dropping on the floor. Ward was a really, really nice guy. Then there was Archie Bunker, who rarely spoke to Edith in anything lower than a shout—and regardless of the volume, his voice was *always* filled with condescension and biting sarcasm.

More contemporary examples include guys like Al Bundy and Homer Simpson, whose "leadership" was known only to them. They lived in their own little fantasy lands of power. But to Peggy Bundy, Marge Simpson, and the rest of their families, these guys were losers—the targets of well-earned ridicule and countless jokes. Or there's Raymond Barone—more interested in his own comfort and in keeping the peace than in effectively leading and loving his family.

But there are other examples—Jesus Christ, for instance. The apostle Paul wrote this enduring description:

> Do nothing out of selfish ambition or vain conceit, but in humility consider others better than yourselves. Each of you should look not only to your own interests, but also to the interests of others.
>
> Your attitude should be the same as that of Christ Jesus:

Who, being in very nature God,
    did not consider equality with God something to
        be grasped,
but made himself nothing,
    taking the very nature of a servant,
    being made in human likeness.
And being found in appearance as a man,
    he humbled himself
    and became obedient to death—
        even death on a cross.

PHILIPPIANS 2:3–8

Jesus was God. He had more power than any man who ever walked the earth's surface, yet his life was a flawless example of the kind of leadership you need to take with your wife. In fact, Jesus commanded it:

> You know that the rulers of the Gentiles lord it over them, and their high officials exercise authority over them. *Not so with you.* Instead, whoever wants to become great among you *must* be your servant, and whoever wants to be first *must* be your slave—just as the Son of Man did not come to be served, but to serve, and to give his life as a ransom for many.

MATTHEW 20:25–28, italics mine

Servanthood is the heart of leadership in your marriage.

Husbands who demand that their wives submit to them have missed the point of leadership altogether. They are like the cartoon king who stomps around the castle screaming, "*I'm* in charge around here!" Men who act this way are only revealing their own insecurity. They're afraid that if they don't make angry demands, no one will follow them.

"Not so with you," Jesus said.

Your most important role is to love your bride as Jesus loved his followers. And how did he do that? By serving. Sacrificing himself. Giving up his rights as the leader. Dying. God's word to us is this: "Husbands, love your wives, just as Christ loved the church and gave himself up for her."[14]

Here's what this kind of leadership might look like in your marriage:

- You and your wife are on your way to dinner. You've not discussed this with your bride, but you're headed for your favorite Mexican place. All day long you've had visions of cheese enchiladas dancing in your head. And this restaurant makes the best enchiladas this side of Tijuana. You turn to your wife, hoping for the "right" answer to the following question: "What sounds good to you tonight?"

   "It's funny," she says. "I've been craving Italian food since breakfast."

   Where do you go to dinner?

- You're backing out of the garage when your wife says something about its condition. This isn't the first time she's asked you to clean it out. You know she's right; it *is* a mess — but the first thing that flashes into your mind is the condition of her sink and vanity in the bathroom.

   What do you say?

Ironically, being a leader in your marriage *is* about you being first. It's about being the first to adjust in order to demonstrate love for your wife. It means being the first in serving, the first in forgiving, and the first in yielding your conveniences.

(Something to ponder: Military officers are the first ones up in the morning and the last ones to bed at night.)

Christian Leadership Concepts (CLC) is an increasingly popular Bible study program for men. Founded by Hal Haddon, a Nashville businessman, this two-year course includes a unit that helps men understand their role as spiritual leaders in their homes. The wives of the men in this course love it when their husbands are going through this section. Why? Is it because their husbands come home and start telling them how they need to get with the program? Of course not. Women love this component because their husbands start loving them in the same radical and sacrificial way that Jesus does.

When Mike Hyatt and I were drawing up the corporate documents for Wolgemuth & Hyatt Publishers, we decided—at the strong advice of our attorney—to make the ownership of the company 51/49 percent and not 50/50. Because I was a little older and had a few more years of publishing experience under my belt, Mike suggested that I take the larger share of ownership. I agreed. But at that moment—I'll never forget it—I made a quiet resolution never to put myself in a position of lording my 51 percent over the 49 percent my business partner held. My job was to cover some of the more cumbersome tasks of the business and to help him develop his skills and gifts. I never told him about this decision. My success was going to show up as his success.

You're the leader—a 51 percent "owner"—in your marriage. That's your role. It's what your wife would choose. Now your most important task should be crystal clear.

You Are a Warrior

When I was a little boy, my parents had a strict "no guns" policy. You never saw my brothers or me with toy-gun holsters hanging from our belts. But what my father and mother didn't realize was that we could make do with a banana, a stick, a pencil, a telephone, a piece of uncooked spaghetti, a sleeping cat, a young sibling, a finger, a stuffed animal—you get the idea.

Aggression is indelibly inscribed into every man. We love to conquer. This desire to do battle comes in different forms. We can spend our lives productively performing our way up the corporate ladder, battling an opponent in the courtroom, winning a local tennis tournament, or combating disease in the operating room. But men who don't give voice to their warrior role in healthy ways will, more often than not, find themselves fighting the wrong battles.

Misguided Battles

- Kimberly walked into the counselor's office and began to unpack her story of loneliness and frustration. Even though she had only been married for a few months, she wept as she talked about how Ryan spends two to three hours a day in the gym but not a fraction of that time working on his marriage.
- Will thinks nothing of investing fifteen hours a week and thousands of dollars a year on his golf game. Betty is angry and confused when Will tells her that they just can't afford a date night—dinner and a movie—every week.
- Mitch would rather volunteer at church than spend time with his wife, Cindy. In fact, instead of treating his wife to breakfast in bed on their anniversary, he shows up at church to flip pancakes at the weekly prayer breakfast.

These warriors are fighting the wrong battles. And even though they didn't set out to destroy their marriages with "friendly fire," it's exactly what they're doing. Kimberly, Betty, and Cindy long for husbands who are strong enough to keep their promises and valiant enough to battle against those habits and attitudes that threaten to destroy their marriages.

You and I come from a long line of strong men who go lifeless in the face of threats to our marriages. This is a tradition that goes all the way back to Adam. Often in Bible studies on the first chapters of Genesis, some guy will quip that it was Eve who gave in to temptation and ate the forbidden fruit. But take a closer look. Where was Adam when the serpent was wooing Eve? He was likely right there next to her. And what did he do when she was beginning to cave in to Satan's lie? Nothing. A classic prototype of the passive man, Adam stood quietly by. When he could have fought for her and defended her against what they both knew was wrong, his lips turned to stone.

We were made for more than this. Your bride may not be a damsel to rescue from a prison tower, but that doesn't mean that there *isn't* a battle to be fought and won on her behalf. This struggle is even more challenging than sculpting your stomach, lowering your handicap, or feeding breakfast to the men at church. And it's more rewarding than any of these things.

You Are a Lover

Living in Central Florida means being surrounded by a lot of people who speak a language other than English—mostly Spanish. It can be pretty frustrating—for them and me—trying to figure out what each of us is saying.

Sometimes my words to my wife are misunderstood. It's almost as though I'm using the wrong dialect. We need to work on our "love language."[15] I think my love for her is best expressed one way—gifts, trips, shopping sprees—but she sees it completely differently. My love for her is most powerfully expressed when I give her time, tenderness, and my undivided attention—when I determine to be a vital part of our two-person "sailing expedition."

Patrick Morley, best-selling author of *The Man in the Mirror,* tells of his quest to learn his wife's love language. One evening, after dinner, instead of excusing himself to finish the newspaper, Patrick tried Patsy's "vernacular." He thanked her for the delicious dinner, stood up, and began to clear the table. Then he offered to put the leftovers into the refrigerator and didn't leave the kitchen until everything was cleaned up and put away. Patrick didn't make any grand announcements about what he was doing. He simply worked alongside his wife, continuing their dinner conversation until the work was done.

The next night he did exactly what he had done the night before, again with no fanfare. For two weeks Patrick did this. Neither one of them said anything about it. One morning as Patrick walked into the bathroom to shave, there on his mirror was a yellow Post-it note: "Patrick, thanks for being my best friend. Love, Patsy." Patrick had learned to speak her language—and adopted the habit of sharing the kitchen duty.

Several years ago, Bobbie began to use an expression when I'd do something she appreciated. "That counts," she'd say with a smile. As I look back on the things that earned this response, I've discovered something interesting about being a lover. The way I keep score of what counts and the way my bride keeps score are vastly different.

As a man, the way I calculate value goes something like this:

- take out the trash—.05 points
- early morning conversation over a cup of coffee—6 points
- dinner and a movie—50 points
- flowers for a birthday or anniversary—125 points
- a weekend at the Ritz in Naples—2,000 points
- jewelry—one point for every dollar spent

Bobbie does appreciate all these things—like I said, they "count." But Bobbie's scoring system works like this:

- take out the trash—1 point
- early morning conversation over a cup of coffee—1 point
- dinner and a movie—1 point
- flowers for a birthday or anniversary—1 point
- a weekend at the Ritz in Naples—1 point
- jewelry—1 point, regardless of the cost

Just the other day I heard about a husband who learned about this point system the hard way. Early one morning, as he was running out the door to work—earlier than usual—his wife stopped him to ask why they weren't having their usual morning cup of coffee together. He told her of a project he hadn't been able to finish the night before and the urgency of getting it done before an important meeting at 9:00 A.M.

"But we *always* start our day together," she said.

"Look," he said, "you and I are going to have a great getaway weekend soon. We'll get caught up then."

The husband thought that a weekend rendezvous at a fabulous hotel—six weeks down the road—would compensate for a missed conversation today. That's because his scoring system was calibrated incorrectly.

This was the reality:

- weekend getaway at a beach resort—1 point
- fifteen minutes of conversation with my wife before going to work—1 point

BECOMING FLUENT

After ten years of marriage and three kids, best-selling author John Ortberg tells how he discovered a nuance of the love language of his wife, Nancy. At bedtime John took over the job of bathing the children. Not only was this a genuine convenience for a very tired mom, but Nancy confessed that watching her husband lean over the tub and scrub the children was a real turn-on for her.

"My kids," John said with a big smile, "were the cleanest kids in the neighborhood."

If you and I are going to be great lovers, the most powerful demonstration of that love will always be in our ability to communicate love in the language our wives understand—both big and little expressions. And once we learn how our brides tally the results, we can begin to keep score the way they do.

Being a charming sexual partner is only a very small part of being a lover who knows how to satisfy his wife. For her to believe that she's married to a great lover, your wife needs to be *known* by you.[16] You must become fluent in her distinct language. Created in the image of God as she is, your wife—like God—loves to be pursued, to be delighted in, to be sought after. She longs to know that she is captivating, cherished, and chosen, not just that you consider her to be "a trooper" or "solid" or "hardworking." And she looks uniquely and exclusively to you to *know* her in this way.

You *can* do this, sailor!

6

TALK: CONVERSATIONAL FOREPLAY

The key to reviving or divorce-proofing a relationship is not in how you handle disagreements but in how you are with each other when you're not fighting. Once the marriage gets "set" at a certain degree of positivity, it will take far more negativity to harm your relationship than if your "set point" were lower.

JOHN GOTTMAN, *THE SEVEN PRINCIPLES*
FOR MAKING MARRIAGE WORK

————◆◆◆◆◆————

One day Allen Lange drove to the airfield after lunch to take a quick spin in his airplane. Walking around the Cessna 182 to unfasten the tie-downs, Allen carefully examined the airplane. Even though he was only eighteen years old, no one would ever accuse him of being sloppy about safety.

With everything in order—including the fuel tanks topped off—Allen crawled into the cockpit, fastened his seat belt, slipped his headset over his ears, and pulled the choke. "Ignition," he whispered, turning the key.

In less than three minutes the tower cleared Allen Lange's plane for takeoff. Gathering speed, he lifted from the runway. It was a perfect day to fly. He was less than ten minutes from the airfield when a loud, popping sound came from the instrument panel directly in front of him. Smoke came pouring from somewhere behind the panel, just above his knees. Allen instinctively cracked open his window to let the smoke exit and turned the plane toward home.

Reaching up to the radio controls, Allen called to the tower: "Cessna 5J644 to Jackson tower. Come in, Jackson—I've got a fire here. Come in, Jackson."

No answer.

Allen adjusted the frequency on his radio. A gust of wind pushed his plane sharply to the left, and Allen pulled back on the stick to compensate. The acrid smell of an electrical fire filled the cockpit.

Allen changed the frequency on his radio. "Cessna 5J644 to Jackson tower. Come in, Jackson. Cessna 5J644 to Jackson tower. I'VE GOT A FIRE HERE. COME IN, JACKSON."

Allen was lost. The smoke inside made it difficult to see his instruments. Worst of all, there was silence. Try as he might to find the correct frequency to reach the tower, there was nothing.

"Talk to me," Allen said out loud, staring at his taciturn radio. "TALK TO ME!" he repeated in a shout. "I'M DYING IN HERE!"

CAN WE TALK?

In this chapter, you and I are going to talk about talking. Before we go any further, though, there are a few things that need to be confessed. First, you and I are probably not very good at talking. In fact, chances are we're downright miserable at it. And second, if your wife is even close to normal, she will sometimes be feeling like Allen Lange at two thousand feet. She's desperate, and she's dying in the silence.

73

I ran across this simple true-false quiz a while ago.[17] It's for wives to take, but before you give it to her, go ahead and guess how she'll respond to each of these questions:

1. I know more about sea anemones than I do about my husband's feelings. T or F
2. My husband's priorities seem to be work, sports, his car, the yard, church, and then me. T or F
3. My husband would rather floss with razor wire than discuss our marriage. T or F
4. My husband would rather jam his head on the end of a sharpened pencil than go to counseling. T or F
5. Sometimes I feel alone in this marriage. T or F
6. I feel alone most of the time in this marriage. T or F
7. I can't describe to you how alone I feel in this marriage. T or F
8. I really wish my husband would change in a few areas. T or F
9. My husband is a great person and I love him, but I'm frustrated because he and I don't seem to be on the same team. T or F
10. I'm willing to do just about anything to change our relationship for the better. T or F

Look back over the list again. Do you think your wife might circle *True* for at least one of these questions? More than one? How many more than one?

Running Away

Scott and Monica fell in love in college. Scott had come from a long line of thoughtful and contemplative people—measured people, so to speak. "No need for small talk" was spot-welded to his DNA. Monica was beautiful, warm, effervescent, outgoing, and talkative—all of which Scott loved about Monica—and Monica boasted to her friends that Scott was the strong, silent type—a man who knew exactly who he was and where he was going.

But it didn't take long after their wedding for these two qualities to meet nose to nose. In fact, Monica had a "sinking feeling" on their honeymoon. Scott's emotionless two- or three-word answers to her questions gripped her with a strange sense of loneliness.

Twenty-five years later, I picked up the phone on a Thursday afternoon to check in with Scott. He and I had been neighbors as youngsters in the Illinois town where we had grown up, and our friendship had lasted a lifetime. I loved Scott like a brother, and Bobbie and Monica had become very close friends, so you'll understand why his words broke my heart.

"Monica is leaving me today," Scott said evenly. "Andrew [the youngest of their four children] graduated from high school on Monday. We had a party for him on Tuesday, and I think Monica's leaving me today."

Scott's prediction was perfect. When he arrived home that night from work, he found an empty garage and a note on the kitchen table.

Two years before, at her thirtieth high school reunion, Monica had reconnected with Brent, her first serious boyfriend. They, along with a tableful of old friends, had talked late into the night. Scott had decided not to attend the reunion. He wasn't crazy about traipsing along with his wife and spending the evening with total strangers. Before the night ended, Monica and Brent had exchanged phone numbers and e-mail addresses.

That Thursday afternoon, almost exactly twenty-four months later, Monica packed everything she could fit into her sports car—including her dog—and drove five hundred miles to move in with Brent. Monica was a Christian. A highly decorated grade school teacher, a person who had volunteered to serve countless times in the nursery during worship, someone who had taught Sunday school for years. She had read Bible stories to her two boys and two girls and had prayed with them at bedtime since they were small. She was a nearly flawless mother. A year before packing up her car and her dog, she had celebrated her fiftieth birthday. But now, like a defiant and unbending teenager, Monica was running away.

"My family thinks I'm visiting my hometown for a few days," she e-mailed us a week later. "But I've moved in with Brent. I'm never going back. Never."

And except to return once to gather the things she hadn't been able to pack into her little car the first time, Monica kept her word. She never went back.

From their first year of marriage, Monica was Allen Lange at two thousand feet in a floundering aircraft. Her cockpit was filled with smoke—and for most of their twenty-five years together she had been unable to reach the Jackson tower. Scott hadn't *meant* to be distant or aloof. He truly loved his wife. He just wasn't a natural conversationalist. And, because of the silence, Monica was dying up there.

As far as she was concerned, running away was the only chance she had to survive.

TALKING, NOT NEGOTIATING

He left a desperate message on my machine. "I've got to talk to you," he said. "Soon!"

Stan and I had had many passing conversations in the halls

at church, at wedding receptions, and at funerals. But even though I didn't know why Stan had called, I was certain that, as I drove to the coffee shop for our emergency meeting, this talk would be different.

Although a highly respected lawyer, that day Stan didn't look the part. His eyes were red and swollen, his hair was tousled, and his clothes looked as though they had been dragged from the laundry hamper. He told me that he and Jill had been separated for a month. At first he had assumed they could simply work it out. Up to this point, he had never lost an argument with his wife, and he was sure it would be a matter of time until she "started to think rationally."

But Stan had been wrong, and he was getting desperate. He explained that, although he still had a key to the house and could come and go during the day, he no longer held a key to Jill's heart. He was certain she had changed the lock. Permanently.

"I think I've lost her," Stan said. At this, his countenance broke. His face turned to a flood of tears. "I've been an idiot," he confessed as he described the marriage that could have been. He described how he had, again and again, beaten her down with his words, always "winning" with condescending words of blame or anger. A crack litigator, Stan had taken his courtroom skills into his home. And in the end, he had lost his case.

As he looked back, Stan replayed all the missed opportunities. He recalled times when Jill had approached him with sincere concern about their "communication problem." Stan had ridiculed her. Then he ignored her. When she suggested they visit with a counselor, Stan punished her with days of the silent treatment. When Jill tried tenderly to ask if they could "just talk," he would sarcastically quip, "Okay, you start."

Jill's countenance would drop, and she'd walk away. She rarely argued. She knew better than to try to negotiate with a man who made hundreds of thousands of dollars a year winning at this game. Incredibly, Stan would chalk up these kinds of encounters as victories.

But now, after only a month of separation, Stan saw himself and his estranged wife with stunning clarity. He knew he was no closer to reconciliation than the day he had moved out. His marriage and his children were slipping away. He had no idea what to do, because his habitual refusal to talk to his wife had burned the very bridge he now needed.

Stan was Allen Lange at two thousand feet, frantically searching for the right frequency—and he was dying up there. What made it worse was that Stan was responsible for his emergency—and he knew it.

OFFERING A SAFE PLACE

Author Leo Buscaglia was once asked to judge a contest that honored children who had done good things. A mother submitted a story of her four-year-old son who, at the time, lived next door to an elderly man. Several days earlier, the man's wife had died, and the little boy had walked over to the neighbor's house to cheer him up. Finding the man sitting on a large chair in the living room, the child climbed up on his lap and laid his head against his chest. The man was crying.

When the boy came home, his mother asked, "What did you say to our neighbor?"

"Nothing," the lad responded. "I just helped him cry."

Sometimes the secret to good conversation with your wife is the part where you don't say anything at all. One of your jobs as a husband is to give your wife a safe place—a place where she can be weak or frightened or lonely. Sometimes you may just need to help her cry.

ENDORSEMENTS

Almost every wife I know of loves to hear her husband talk *about* her with unsolicited endorsements spoken in her presence.

Several years ago our daughter Missy told us about a conversation between her husband, Jon, and Jon's Uncle Tom. Tom's wife had lost a battle to cancer, leaving Tom to raise his two small children alone. A very successful businessman, Tom had decided to hire full-time help in caring for his children.

"I've hired a nanny," Tom told Jon. "And she's terrific. Not only are the kids happy, but when I come home from work, I find the house in order. Dinner is ready, the kitchen is clean, even my underwear and socks have magically left the clothes hamper and are folded neatly back in my closet."

Jon's eyes left Tom. He looked at Missy, then back at his uncle. "I know just what you mean," he said with a smile. "I get that every day myself. My home has the same kind of magic."

Missy told me that she held on to those words for months. They provided encouragement when she found herself consigned to mundane chores like laundry. They inspired her and kept her from feeling useless or unimportant. Even though they hadn't been directed at her, Jon's words of endorsement unlocked Missy's heart and deepened her love for her husband.

The late Charlie Shedd, author of several best-selling books on sex and marriage,[18] was one of the happiest married men I've ever known. His secret was a very simple thing. Early in his marriage, Charlie challenged himself to say something kind—a new something he hadn't said before—to Martha every day. His comment may have been a thank you, a kind word about her heart for people, a statement of appreciation for her love for God, or an expression of delight over something she did or said.

When I first met Charlie and Martha, they were well into their third decade of marriage. Martha told me with a smile that there were "very few days" that Charlie hadn't kept his promise. She looked forward to his daily endorsements. And she loved him for his commitment to keep them coming. Charlie was a happily married man because Martha was a happily married woman.[19]

Endorsements work.

Conversation without Destination

Did you know that women don't need a reason for calling each other on the phone? It's true. And not only do they make such calls, they can talk for thirty minutes when both of them know that there was no agenda in the first place. This may be as amazing to you as it is to me—but it's true.

You and I, on the other hand, rarely do such a thing. It can even be difficult to check in with our parents, because we know it'll be one of those conversations without a destination.

More often than not, I'm driven in my conversations to a goal. I call my barber to set up an appointment. "Next Tuesday? 4:30? Got it. Thanks." In my business, I call clients or customers with the same agenda: "You and I know we've got work to do. Let's cut the small talk and get to the point. This call isn't the only one we have on our lists today." We don't actually say these words on business calls, but most of the time it's exactly what's going on.

But now you're a married man. You're going to have to learn that the most important person in your life may want to talk without any sort of strategic plan in mind. She may need some conversation without a destination.

Example 1: A Destination Conversation

> *Your wife:* "You've been so busy that it seems like we don't talk like we used to. We never just sit and talk. It seems like you talk to other people, but you don't talk to me."
>
> *You:* "No problem. Let's talk. Name a subject, and we can talk about it."
>
> *Your wife:* "AAAHHHH! I shouldn't *have* to ask you to talk. I'm your wife. Before we got married we used to stay up till the wee hours of the morning just talking. Now I barely get a grunt out of you."
>
> *You:* "Don't you see what's happening? I can't win. When I don't talk to you, I'm in trouble. When I offer to talk to you, I'm in trouble. I can't win."

What you are missing here is that your bride doesn't want to have a talk that will "accomplish something." She doesn't want to reserve a rental car or make a hotel reservation. This talk does not have a finish line. She just wants to talk.

Example 2: A No-Destination Conversation

Imagine a different strategy on your part:

> *Your wife:* "You've been so busy that it seems like we don't talk like we used to. We never just sit and talk. It seems like you talk to other people, but you don't talk to me."
>
> *You:* "You're right. I've been so preoccupied that I've not paid much attention to you recently. I'm sorry. I've got so many things I'd like to tell you about, but why don't you go first. Tell me all about your day."

Your wife: "AAAHHHH! I shouldn't *have* to ask—Wait a minute. What did you say?"

You: "I said, 'You're right, and I want to hear about your day.' "

Your wife: "Well, okay. Hmmm—well, it all started this morning as I was getting ready to walk out the door to go to work. The garbage disposal went out—I couldn't believe it—wait a minute, are you *sure* you want to hear about this?"

You: "Absolutely!"

After your wife finishes talking, she turns to you and asks about *your* day. Do you say, "It was fine. Where's the paper?" No, you say, "Well, I met Ralph for coffee this morning. It looks like Jimmy is going to UVA in the fall. He's applying for a music scholarship at Julliard, but they don't think he's got much of a shot, so they're guessing it's going to be UVA. When I got to the office, the coffee machine had gone berserk and there was an inch of standing water in the workroom. Nancy had already called maintenance, but the water was already seeping into the carpet in the reception area. Stephanie announced that she's pregnant and that she's going to stay home once the baby's born . . ."

Get the idea? For your bride, it's not so much *what* you talk about but *the fact that you talk* that makes the real difference.

One of the reasons we chicken out of agendaless conversations is our fear of not having something significant to cover. Something profound (like a change in the weather patterns) or something measurable (like last night's basketball scores). Actually, conversations without destinations can be wonderful. In fact, they're like the guys walking up and down the beach slowly swinging their metal detectors. You just never know what treasure you might find.

The other reason for learning how to meet your wife's needs in good conversation is that she's absolutely desperate for it—just as panicked as Allen Lange was when he couldn't connect with the traffic control tower. For her it's almost a matter of life and death.

Bobbie and I are working on our fourth decade of marriage. And I wish I could tell you that these destinationless conversations are effortless. They aren't. However, they *are* easier than they used to be. If you stay with it long enough, I promise that it will get easier.

WHERE'S ALLEN?

"Cessna, this is Jackson tower, come in! We've got you in our sights. Landing lights are on."

The connection is made. Allen is safe at last.

7

FRIENDSHIP: THE SECRET INGREDIENT IN EVERY SATISFYING MARRIAGE

Let there be times when the conversation is not supposed to be "deep." This is hardly a waste of time. It is marriage. And without it the marriage starts to starve.

WALTER WANGERIN, *AS FOR ME AND MY HOUSE*

I t was late. As I turned into our driveway, my headlights washing across the front of our home like a great wave, I noticed that one of the lamps in the living room was on. *Great*, I naively thought to myself, *Bobbie must still be awake.* I couldn't wait to fill her in on what had just happened.

Pulling the car into our detached garage, I jumped out and ran down the sidewalk, entered the house, and hustled into the living room. Sure enough, Bobbie was sitting on one end of the sofa, next to the end table and lighted lamp. The fact that she was neither watching TV nor had any reading material on her lap should have tipped me off. But we had only been married for a few months, and I wasn't very adept at reading the signs. Plopping down next to her, I eagerly began to tell her about my evening.

At the time, I was employed by a well-known international youth ministry. I had the responsibility of working with students at three local high schools. I coordinated the club meetings held in kids' homes and did lots of one-on-one counseling. On this particular night, I was bursting with the news that one of "my kids" had decided to turn his life around. He had been a heavy drug user, and his parents had threatened to send him away to get help. Then I had come along, befriended the young man, and, by the grace of God, had actually motivated him to clean up his act.

On and on I went, telling Bobbie the story.

Now, remember that I was new at the marriage thing. I didn't notice that Bobbie wasn't celebrating the good news. The cool breeze emanating from her end of the couch should have told me something, but this was about *me* and *my* story, so I rode it all the way to the end.

I waited for Bobbie's response. There was nothing. Only then did I look squarely into her eyes, and it dawned on me that she may have heard the words but really hadn't been listening. Even though it happened a long time ago, I can tell you exactly what she said in the end. These were her first words—uttered with no change in facial expression—following my nonstop success report: "I don't care."

I was stunned.

"You don't care?" I said in my best shame-on-you, guilt-inducing voice. "You don't care?"

"No, I don't," she said, her steely green eyes leaving no doubt. "You're late," she continued. "You told me you'd be home by 9:00, and you didn't even have the courtesy to call me. You're spending all your waking hours with those kids, and this isn't the *first* time you've come home later than you promised. Where do *I* fit in?"

I didn't say anything. It was my turn to be silent.

"You're out there saving the whole world. And I'm home alone, waiting for you—and I'm sick of it!"

There are no words to adequately describe my utter shock at that moment. I had never heard a wife talk to her husband like this. (It wasn't one of my *normals*.) I remember thinking—because my self-centeredness was off the charts—that I had made a terrible mistake in marrying this wild woman.

More than thirty years have passed since that awful night. Bobbie and I have learned how to speak words more clearly and with a little less bite. But I know exactly what she was telling me. It was, in reality, a very simple truth—a truth that had nothing to do with disdain for the young people I was working with (she loved them as much as I did) or her own spiritual condition (she loves God and is a living example of his grace everywhere she goes). Here's what Bobbie was saying to me. It's a powerful thing and one of the reasons why that night was one of the most significant turning points in our marriage: "I'm your wife. But I also want to be your friend. You'd never treat a friend like this."

Of course, it took years (literally) for us to completely unpack what Bobbie was feeling that night. But I am so thankful she had the courage, very early in our marriage, to try to tell me the truth—and to express her expectations—about our relationship. She didn't just want to be married to me. She wanted us to be friends.

Sometimes, "walking down the aisle" changes the bride and groom from good friends into lovers only. This change can only be described as extremely dangerous—and in every case, it's relationship-threatening.

A PROFOUNDLY SIMPLE TRUTH

Over the past decade, Dr. John Gottman, a University of Washington professor, has taken a number of the most widely accepted assumptions about marriage and turned them on their ear. He's one of the only researchers in the field of marriage studies who has brought rigorous scientific methods to bear on predicting what makes marriages work and what makes them fail.

After detailed interviews with a couple, Dr. Gottman actually observes them in what has become known as his "love lab." With precision, Gottman and his colleagues have developed a process of watching married couples and pinpointing hundreds of specific behaviors.

Each couple is allowed to "live normally" in a nicely furnished apartment outfitted with video cameras, one-way glass, and microphones in every room except the bedroom and bathroom. Holter monitors are worn by each of the participants.[20] Then, from 9:00 A.M. until 9:00 P.M., they are carefully observed.

After years of surveillance and analysis of hundreds of couples, Gottman claims to be able to predict the future success or failure of a marriage with an accuracy rate of over 90 percent. And usually his conclusions are drawn within just five minutes of observation.[21]

You're undoubtedly thinking, *How does he do it?* Dr. Gottman has identified specific behaviors that are marriage destroyers and others that are marriage protectors. Far and away, the *most* significant marriage protector boils down to one word (are you ready to be underwhelmed?): *friendship.* Not money, not exotic getaways, not creative romantic rendezvous. No, merely friendship. Gottman makes this observation:

The determining factor in whether wives feel satisfied with sex, romance, and passion in their marriage is, by 70 percent, the quality of the couple's friendship. For men, the determining factor is, by the same 70 percent, the quality of the couple's friendship. So men and women come from the same planet after all. . . . Friendship fuels the flames of romance because it offers the best protection against feeling adversarial toward your spouse.[22]

There's very good news for you and me in this discovery. Successful marriage may not require us to learn anything new. Building a friendship with your wife early in your marriage is a matter of accessing skills you learned as a youngster. You know the rules. You know what it takes to find a friend and to keep one. All you have to do is to apply this knowledge to the most important relationship you have.

More Control Than We Think

Let's pretend that you and your wife are locked in a heated argument. Words are loud and biting. Maybe there are some tears. Then the phone rings. You reach to answer it. "Hello," you say in such a friendly voice that the caller may think you were watching a ball game on TV when the phone rang. It's a close friend. The conversation isn't a long one, and although your wife cannot hear the other person, she hears the tone of your voice. She also realizes how quickly you were able to switch its timbre when you realized who it was that called. You did it instantly with your voice—and your attitude—because you chose to do so.

Some husbands and wives assume that, when it comes to conflicts with each other, they "just can't help" but speak to each other with disrespect and unkindness. But it's not true. We *can* help it. In fact, we *always* find the resources to speak respectfully and kindly to those whose friendship or business we value enough—and this should, obviously, include our wives.

But there is more to friendship than just avoiding negative dialogue.

JUST NORMAL STUFF

Treating your wife like a friend includes engaging in conversations that may not be dramatic at all. Consider this example:

You walk into the kitchen early on a crisp autumn Saturday morning. Your wife is already up, standing at the window with a cup of coffee in her hand. You find the newspaper on the kitchen counter, sit down, and pour yourself some coffee.

> *Your wife (gazing out the window):* "Look at those leaves. Aren't they incredible?"
>
> *You (looking up from the paper and glancing out the window where she's standing):* "They sure are." (You follow your comment with an affirming "hmmm" sound.)
>
> *Your wife (still looking out):* "This is my favorite time of the year."
>
> *You (looking at the paper):* "Hey, listen to this!"
>
> *Your wife (turning from the window and walking toward the sink):* "Listen to what?"
>
> *You:* "The Johnsons are finally selling that store."
>
> *Your wife (opening a cabinet):* "No kidding? We thought they'd never sell."
>
> *You (still looking at the paper):* "I guess someone made them an offer they couldn't refuse."

> *Your wife (walking over toward a lamp but pausing before she reaches out to turn it on):* "Could we run to the hardware store this morning? We need to get some lightbulbs."
>
> *You:* "Uh-huh."

Did you catch the theatrics, the tension, the passion?

You're right. It wasn't there. Nothing dramatic. Nothing heroic. But this is the very kind of interchange that can do wonders to build that marriage-protecting friendship. Gottman calls this process "turning toward each other." And he claims that these simple gestures of attentiveness — these casual exchanges — practiced thousands of times throughout your marriage, can build a comfortable friendship that can protect your marriage against the things that could easily destroy it.

The kind of dialogue shown above can happen among friends without any effort. For example, if you and your closest friends were out of town for a weekend golf outing and found yourselves at the breakfast table together early one morning, this kind of conversation would have happened with no effort at all. It bears repeating: the friendship-building skills that you must apply to your marriage are skills you already have in your repertoire.

Compare the conversation pattern of "turning toward each other" to that of a husband who continually ignores his wife. They talk *over* each other, *at* each other, *about* each other, *behind* each other's backs — rarely *with* each other.

But solid friendship includes more than conversation. Sometimes it affects your calendar.

TIME

Something that posed a huge threat early in our marriage was carving away time to spend together. The relentless and unpredictable pace of our lives made it difficult to find enough time to be together. And, given the pressures—most of them urgent—of my life, it was much too easy to assume that Bobbie could wait. The phone call couldn't wait; the airplane couldn't wait; the conference in Dallas couldn't wait. But Bobbie—*she* could wait.

Without the courage to confront the problem and without a willingness to say no to a host of good opportunities, Bobbie and I could have drifted dangerously apart. My decision to take a serious look at my calendar came at Bobbie's insistence. Instinctively she knew that distance would devastate our relationship. She saw the potential dangers, and she was determined not to be distracted from her goal of finding time to be together. Sometimes she made a game out of it—packing a picnic basket and bringing it to the office when I had to work late. Who could resist the checkered tablecloth spread out on the office floor? Sandwiches, potato salad, ice tea—and no ants. I'm thankful because I know the friendship we now enjoy is a result of her relentless pursuit of my calendar.

The Slot System

Mark and Susan's story is very similar to ours. But their approach to reserving enough time for each other was more measured. In fact, early in their marriage, Susan and Mark took a long walk that, according to Mark, put them on a course that saved their marriage. Susan was concerned about the negative effect that the unrelenting demands of ministry could have on their marriage. And so, before the walk ended, she had presented a plan—a simple strategy to protect their marriage from the corrosive effects of too much time apart. Mark was introduced to what they now call the *slot system*. The truth at work here is this: without some kind of planning, your marriage will be ruled (and overruled) by your schedule rather than the other way around.

Since that conversation, Mark has seen two measurable results: (1) Because the slot system worked so effectively, their conflicts about time spent together have been rare, and (2) Mark and Susan have taught this system to hundreds of couples—with rave reviews.

When they teach this system, they begin by dividing a typical week into twenty-one separate slots. It looks like this:

Sunday	Monday	Tuesday	Wednesday	Thursday	Friday	Saturday

Each day has three slots—morning, afternoon, and evening. Mark and Susan concluded that they needed a minimum of six slots together in a normal week. Each slot includes a meal and a block of time. The morning slots begin with breakfast and end before lunch. The afternoon slots begin with lunch and end around 5:00 P.M. Dinner is in the evening slot, which ends at bedtime.

The Slot System—Exhibit A

Let's look at how the slot system worked for Todd and Melanie. Mark had conducted their wedding two years earlier, and now they had made an appointment to see him again. These two had entered marriage with their eyes wide open. They had brought a willingness to do "whatever it takes" to make their marriage thrive. In fact, one of the agreements they had made in premarital counseling was that if their relationship ever got below "excellent," they would make an appointment to see Mark—which is why they were now sitting in Mark's office.

Melanie began. "Something's missing," she said. Todd nodded in agreement. "We married each other because we wanted to dance," she continued. "But it feels like we're just trudging along, trying to make our life together work."

"It's like our car isn't running on all cylinders," Todd offered. "Like our wheels are turning without bearings."

When Mark asked Todd and Melanie how they were doing in making time for each other, they both laughed—almost always a good sign in marriage counseling.

"What's so funny?" Mark asked.

"It's just nuts right now," Todd offered. "What with starting a new business, I'm working late most nights. I typically get home around 8:00 at night. I'm exhausted. And that's when we get into our worst fights."

Mark then asked about weekends.

Melanie explained that Todd was working nearly every Saturday. Most Sundays Melanie led the children's choir at church and Todd helped out with the youth group in the afternoon. "We've been good about having our date night on Saturdays," she concluded. "But lately, there's just been a lot of tension, even when we're doing something fun."

Todd and Melanie had forgotten the one nutrient their marriage most needed: *time together*. Scheduled, *quantity* time together does for a marriage what an oil change does for a car; it guarantees that all the parts of the engine function smoothly with a minimum of wear and tear.

Mark pulled out a blank "slot system" sheet and asked Todd and Melanie to take a look at their upcoming week. "Fill in the things that are already scheduled," Mark said. "Then find six slots where you can be together, even if you have to move some things around. And don't just think of these slots as romantic getaways. They could be taken up with running errands together, watching TV, taking a nap, having dinner together with friends, or just hanging around the house."

As Mark explained the process, Todd and Melanie swallowed hard. They knew their schedule would not easily yield to this kind of demand. While they were pondering, Mark made a few suggestions to Todd. "If you have to work late, instead of working until 8:00 on two nights, why don't you work until 10:00 one night, then come home by 5:30 the next night. That gives you a slot with Melanie. Or, instead of working from 10:00 until 4:00 on Saturday, why don't you go early and work until noon. That'll give you two slots with Melanie on Saturday."

Surprisingly, after only ten minutes of negotiating, Todd and Melanie had come up with this plan for their week:

Sunday	Monday	Tuesday	Wednesday	Thursday	Friday	Saturday
1. Breakfast & church together	**W**	**O**	**R**	**K**	**!**	◯
◯	**W**	**O**	**R**	**K**	**!**	5. Home improvement projects
2. Youth Group at our house	◯	3. Dinner at home	◯	◯	4. Dinner with John and Louise	6. Date night

Once they had picked their six slots and numbered them from 1 to 6, Mark drew five circles in their schedule. "Part of the beauty of this system," he explained, "is that it not only gives you an appropriate amount of time *together*, it also provides you with pockets of freedom for each of you to plan your *own* activities—without feeling guilty or pressured to beg for permission from each other."

The circles in this schedule represent times when you and your wife are free to work a few extra hours or plan an independent activity—going to a sporting event with friends, enrolling in an art class, or whatever. With this plan, you'll achieve a good balance between sufficient time together and guilt-free time apart. You'll find yourself protected from feeling smothered by too much time with each other or alienated by not having enough.

Whenever Mark teaches the slot system, someone invariably asks about those times when six slots a week are simply impossible—out-of-town business trips, unforeseen crises at work, and the like. He acknowledges that this happens to him regularly. However, he goes on to make a critical point—one I'd encourage you not to miss. Mark and Susan have determined that by making six slots their norm, their marriage is well prepared to handle those times when six slots just aren't going to happen in a given week. "We have chosen," they explain, "to set the default button on six, so that it's *normal* to have enough time together and *abnormal* to miss each other for a whole week."

Pay attention now. Here's the most important thing Mark says about the slot system: "Give up on the myth of *quality time* with your wife. Trying to squeeze *quality* out of an hour or two a week is going to be an exercise in frustration. But carving out specific blocks of *quantity* time is always the most fertile ground for growing *quality* time in your marriage."

THE ZERO-SECRETS POLICY

My grandparents' house smelled. It wasn't an overpowering stench; it was just enough that when we'd visit, it would greet us like an unfriendly host. When my grandparents entered a rest home, the new owners of their house made a complete renovation—and I'm convinced that one of the reasons was to get rid of the smell.

Untold secrets often become a stench that hides in the walls of your marriage. You can't see it, but you both know that something "smells" wrong. We say to engaged couples that if they can't handle revealing secrets when they're in the thick of romance, they surely won't be able to handle it when the protective buffers around their marriage have worn thin.

The seeds that can later sprout and destroy marriages usually hide in secrets:

- the female friend at work in whom you confide
- the job you lost because you got caught stealing
- the secret e-mail address your bride doesn't know about
- the fact that you cheated your way through school
- the quantity of alcohol you consume when she's not around
- the pornography you view on a regular basis

When we suggest that couples adopt a zero-secrets policy, someone (usually the guy) often asks, "Are you saying that I need to tell my wife every time I lust after another woman?"

Our answer is a resounding, "Sort of."

Your wife doesn't need to get a catalog of every lustful thought you have, but telling her that this is something you struggle with will shed light on it and release it from your secret memory bank—and it will also create accountability.

Twenty years ago I worked on the second floor of a new office building. My desk faced the front window overlooking the parking lot. Early one day, I looked up from my desk in time to see a woman walking from her car into the building. She looked like a model. Her face and her body were flawless. Her stride was silky and strong. My heart raced as I watched her until she disappeared into the building directly under my window.

Wow, I thought to myself, *I wonder who THAT is.*

The next morning, quite by accident, something caught my eye again. I looked up and saw the same woman walking from her car. My eyes did not leave her until she was out of sight once more. For the next few mornings, the woman's appearance was no longer a surprise. I watched for her. I waited for her. I stood at the window to get a better look. During the day, my mind would drift back to her. I began to think about how I might meet her — perhaps wait for her and act as though I was leaving the building as she approached. I had allowed my mind to go too far. I had crossed the line, and I knew it.

"I've got to tell you something," I said to Bobbie the next weekend. "There's a woman I see walking into the building every day . . ."

For the next few minutes, I explained what had happened and how this mystery woman had captured my imagination. The burden of keeping a secret from Bobbie was more than I wanted to carry. I told her that I was sorry and needed her forgiveness for my foolishness. She thanked me for telling her and willingly forgave me.

By the way, although I noticed the woman on Monday morning, my eyes left her before she made it to the front door. Because I had told Bobbie, the thrill of watching was gone.

Secrets that hide can fester and become serious infections inside your marriage. They have the power to ruin your friendship. They need air in order to heal.

One Last Thought about Secrets

Your wife may have secrets of her own that need to be shared with you. These are secrets you may not want to know about, but they're secrets she may need to tell you. Telling you about these will relieve the burden she's been carrying—the burden of hiding something from you. When she does tell you, she will need your words of assurance, your forgiveness, your affection—and not your judgment.

8

CONFLICT: ONLY YOU CAN PREVENT FOREST FIRES

Aravis and Shasta got so used to fighting and making up again that they decided to get married so as to do it more conveniently.

C. S. LEWIS, *THE HORSE AND HIS BOY*

Although the fire station was all the way downtown Wheaton, Illinois, I could hear the sirens the moment they started wailing. I suppose my ears were particularly attuned that afternoon, because the fire trucks were coming to see me.

When I was a kid, long before the concept of recycling ever hit the scene, we separated our trash. The purpose, however, was not to recycle it but to burn it! There were two huge washing machine boxes in the garage—one was for tin cans and glass, the other for "burnable scrap." Then every two or three weeks, one of the boys—my three brothers or I—was charged with wrestling the box onto our Red Flyer wagon for the short trip to the "way back" to be burned. (Actually, unlike mowing the grass or cleaning the basement floor, this wasn't a chore I dodged.)

On this particular day, my brother—I was twelve, and he was five—came along. It was better to have someone walk along to help steady the oversized box on top of the undersized wagon.

When we reached the burning area, Danny and I turned the box over and dumped its contents. We hadn't noticed the wind until the box was empty and we had to chase a few wayward pieces of paper that skittered into the tall grass. I asked Danny to stand guard in case any burning papers made it over to the tall grass, and then I lit the fire. So far, so good. But once the stack of stuff was engulfed in flames, I got to thinking, *I wonder what would happen if I took some of this fire and laid it next to the tall grass.*

"Don't do it," Danny warned when he saw what I was doing. *What do little brothers know?* I thought to myself.

"You'll start a big fire," he said, his eyes widening. "I'll tell Mother." (The ultimate little brother warning.)

I was unaffected by my brother's words—and so, given the wind and the dry conditions, we had a for-real prairie fire going in no time at all. At first, the grass fire was very small, not too much for our stamping and stomping. Then I held my little brother back for a brief moment, just to let the fire get bigger. More interesting. At that moment we both realized that we were no longer in control.

Spotting the flames from the kitchen window, my mother called the fire department—the number was dutifully taped to the wall telephone (remember, there were *four* boys living here). Then she grabbed a bucket from under the sink, filled it as quickly as she could, and ran to the blazing field. In order to help her run more swiftly, she held the bucket in her arms rather than at her side, the water violently sloshing back and forth.

Just as I looked up to see my mother running toward me, she tripped on a stick and fell headlong onto the grass. The bottom of the bucket slammed against the hard ground and the water shot straight up like a geyser, then it returned to earth, soaking her from head to toe.

Although my dad traveled around the world for a living, he wasn't far *enough* away at that moment—I think he was in Greece—because I got what was coming to me when he returned. I might have been able to avoid a spanking, given the dry and windy conditions, had it not been for Danny's truthful report. My attempt to bribe him only made it worse. (By the way, when I told my story to Mark, he laughed and told me about the first time the fire trucks showed up to put out *his* prairie fire—he was ten years old. What is it about boys and matches anyway?)

Where There's Smoke . . .

It probably didn't take long after you and your bride walked down the aisle until you learned something about your marriage. Your arguments didn't go away. You had some when you were engaged, and you hoped that getting married would put an end to them—at least to their frequency and intensity. How wrong could you have been?

You've been able to control some of these conflicts, but like our youthful pyro-experiences, a few have gotten completely out of control. Smoke has been visible for miles. And when it happens, you and your bride may take on the characteristics of one of these five animals. See if you can identify yourself—and her.

An Ostrich

When the conflict escalates beyond a casual disagreement, the ostrich puts his head in the sand. *This isn't happening,* he lies to himself as he walks away from his wife. Picking up the remote, he clicks on the television, hoping to find something that will drown out his wife's voice—especially if she's . . .

A Tiger

This is the classic winner-take-all fighter. At the first sight of an escalating fight, her fangs glisten and her claws extend. The way to get the upper hand in this fight is to injure the opponent, and the longer she's married to him, the easier it is to find just the right words to hurt him. Of course, ignoring a tiger only escalates her fury, like if she's married to . . .

A Turtle

At first glance, this husband looks like an ostrich, but don't be fooled. His head only pulls back into his shell until just the right moment, and then it darts out and snaps vicious and hurtful words. When his wife fights back, his head has disappeared again. Of course, even if his head is tucked back into his shell, there isn't much comfort if he's married to . . .

A Skunk

Agile and cunning, this fighter—with or without intent—stirs up a fight, then sprays its victim with a barrage of awful and often unrelated generalizations. The skunk may run from the argument, slam doors, or even shout from the other room, but there's a hint of sport in this fighter. It's almost as though she enjoys the smell she creates. Of course, the only way the skunk can feel guilty about leaving such horrible odors behind is if she's married to . . .

A Puppy

Anger is almost invisible on this person's menu of emotions. His favorite retorts are "whatever" and "it's no big deal." He often tries to avoid the issue by saying something he thinks is funny. He hates fights and will do anything to keep peace, but sometimes he creates messes that have to be cleaned up by someone else. Even if it means taking all the blame, his goal is to keep a disagreement from escalating into something unfriendly.

TURNING SKIRMISHES INTO STEPPING-STONES

After years of marriage, observation of other couples, and counseling experiences, we've come up with some strategies that have helped to tame these nasty animals—or to use the earlier imagery, some tactics to help keep the fire sirens from going off. These have not prevented small blazes from springing up now and then; but by and large they've kept them from escalating to the point where our home—and the neighbor's homes—became threatened by the carnage.

In fact, for some men, these strategies have successfully turned skirmishes into stepping-stones, helping their marriages go from ordinary to great.

Fire Safety Strategy #1: Embrace Imperfection

The foundation for this strategy begins with a false expectation. You had it when you got married, and your wife had it, too. Don't worry, it's a hope shared by nearly every bride and groom, and it goes something like this: "I love this person very much, but there are a *few* things that need to be adjusted in her personality and habits. I'll get to those just as soon as we're married."

Oh, and here's another dream shatterer: "Our relationship is meant to be. God brought us together—so when we get married, we won't fight."

If you had been fortunate enough to marry a perfect, sinless woman, these hopes may have been possible. Or if she had been that lucky in marrying a perfect you, these dreams may have also come true. But neither of these things happened. You and your bride came from the ranks of the imperfect, and you both married out of the same flawed inventory.

I've spent most of my career in the publishing business, which means that I have read—or scanned—thousands of manuscripts over the course of the past thirty years. One of the things I've noticed is that my immediate focus is on the mistakes in the work, not on the good that's there. Being a skillful editor is a good thing for me professionally. But in my marriage, focusing on my wife's problems and making note of them—especially with a red pen—spells big trouble.

Ironically, after twenty years in the business, I stepped out to write my first book. And when I received my manuscript back from my editor, I discovered red marks everywhere. At that moment I realized *my own* need to be edited and the pain my editing had inflicted on others.

Since you also recognize imperfection in yourself (at least I hope you do), this strategy is best implemented with a non-verbal acknowledgement to yourself that being married to you must be hard work. Since we all struggle with self-centeredness, this can be a pretty tough admission. But once you've silently made peace with your own flaws, it will be easier to admit them to your wife, even during an argument.

"You're right," you could say when she accuses you of messing up. "You're right, and I shouldn't have done—or said—that." You cannot imagine how effective this can be in helping extinguish the early flames.

Dr. Henry Brandt, one of the pioneers in the field of Christian counseling, discovered a secret weapon in helping married couples come to terms with their inevitable differences. Dr. Brandt would begin his initial session by asking a single question, first to the husband and then to the wife: "Before we start on your list of grievances with each other, I would like to know—what do you need to confess?"

The recognition of your own imperfections opens the door to understanding your wife's flaws. Believe it or not, when you take this as a challenge, you may be better at it than she is, so it's appropriate for you to go first.

I'm not much of a sailor, but I've come to know one of the basic laws of avoiding tragedy on the sea: The ship that can maneuver the easiest should yield to the less nimble craft. As you begin to disclose your own imperfections, your wife will feel safe in unveiling her own.

Fire Safety Strategy #2: You Can Disagree without Fighting

Just because it's natural—and healthy—for you and your wife to have conflicts and disagreements, it doesn't mean that these *have* to turn into fights. Dr. John Gray, of Mars and Venus fame, says that heated arguments are not a helpful way of dealing with disagreement. The problem is that fighting turns the focus toward "defending and winning" and away from solving the issue at hand.

During our first year of marriage, Bobbie and I discovered that there were things we said during our disagreements that could immediately infuriate each other, escalating the discussion into a blazing prairie fire. So we took a bold step. During a calm discussion following one of these battles, we sat down to discuss our own private "rules of engagement."

The Geneva Convention

On June 24, 1859, Henri Dunant[23] witnessed the Battle of Solferino in northern Italy. Seeing the bloodshed, Dunant immediately began enlisting local peasants to carry the wounded from the battlefield and take them to local churches, where doctors tried to relieve their suffering.

Deeply troubled by the inhumane treatment of wounded soldiers, Dunant and four other men organized an international conference of thirteen nations in Geneva, Switzerland, to discuss ways to make warfare more "humane." At the end of the conference on August 22, 1864, the representatives had signed the Geneva Convention. This agreement provided for the neutrality of ambulances and military hospitals, the protection of people who helped the wounded, and the return of prisoners to their country. It also adopted the use of a white flag with a red cross on hospitals, ambulances, and evacuation centers—whose neutrality would be recognized by this symbol.

Even though the Geneva Convention has gone through several revisions in the past 150 years—including the denunciation of chemical weapons in battle—it has stood like a sentry over hundreds of battles. And tens of thousands of soldiers have been saved because of its protection.

During our first year of marriage, Bobbie and I agreed that the inevitable clashes in our marriage should be under the protection of our own "Geneva Convention." And so we decided on the following nonnegotiables—situations where we'd *never* mistreat the wounded or use mustard gas:

> 1. *We will not criticize each other in public (including—some day—in the presence of our kids).* When one of us has been hurt by the other, the victim will come directly to the spouse as soon as possible in private, explaining his or her perspective.
>
>   *Do say (while driving home from a party):* "What you said to your friends about my eating habits really hurt my feelings. It's unfair, and it embarrassed me."

Do not say to your wife (while standing with your friends at the party): "Isn't that your third trip to the buffet? Haven't you had enough?"

2. *We will not address areas of disagreement when we're at our worst.* Bobbie and I learned that serious discussions are rarely well served when we're exhausted from a busy day or when we're not feeling well—emotionally or physically. Our condition usually made a pointed conversation more frustrating, and we rarely reached a solution.

   Do say: "I'm eager to talk about this as soon as we can, but I know we're both very tired. I don't think it's a good time to try to deal with this issue. Let's talk about it over coffee in the morning. Please don't forget that I love you—but right now we both need to get some rest."

   Do not say: "I don't care how you feel. The Bible says, 'Don't let the sun go down on your wrath.' Well the sun is down, and I'm ticked. And would you *please* quit crying."

3. *We will not resort to name-calling.* This includes referring to each other by our parents' first names. (Maybe you've discovered that your wife and her mother share some of the characteristics that most frustrate you.)

   Do say: "It really bugs me when you do that."

   Do not say: "Nice going, 'Geraldine.' "

4. *We will not, in the heat of the battle, bring up information shared in moments of sincere vulnerability.* From the time you and your wife decided that marriage was where you wanted to end up, you engaged in intimate conversations about your deepest fears, regrets, or failures. Arguments are out-of-bounds for the retrieval and regurgitation of this information.

   Do say: "I know how angry this kind of thing makes you. I'm sorry you feel this way."

   Do not say: "What else would I expect from the granddaughter of an alcoholic?"

5. *We will not use each other's physical characteristics as ammunition when we're arguing.* As with references to intimate secrets or making unfair comparisons to each other's parents, unkind comments about our bodies are forbidden.

   Do say . . . absolutely nothing about this.

   Do not say: "Keep your big, fat, knobby German nose out of my business."

These are the articles of our Geneva Convention. And whether you borrow some from us or start from scratch, having your own list is going to keep your battles inbounds. Because, as a man, you're wired to compete and win at war, it's going to be tough to refrain from using your "trump cards." But don't succumb to the temptation. They're chemical weapons. Please don't use them.

Here's the way we monitor our Geneva Convention: if any of the rules are broken, the offending party immediately loses the argument. It's over—on the spot. I'd encourage the same kind of inflexibility in your marriage.

Fire Safety Strategy #3: Try the Instruction Manual

The Bible has a few specific and unambiguous directives for you and me. Obeying these will work wonders in keeping your arguments from breaking out into "first year of marriage" bloodshed.

1. **Be considerate, . . . and treat [her] with respect.**[24] Immediately following this directive, aimed specifically at husbands, is the prospect of a terrible thing that will happen to us if we disobey, namely, that our prayers will be hindered. It's incredible, but true. If you stoop to disrespecting your wife, a lid gets put on your prayer life. It will be as though your prayer "radio" will no longer be tuned to God's station for his leading in other areas of your life. Imagine the devastating consequences of missing God's voice when he speaks to you through circumstances, other people, or his Word.

This passage from 1 Peter goes on to refer to your bride as "the weaker partner." What an interesting thing to say. Here's what it means: The word *weaker* has nothing to do with your wife's tenacity or discipline, or her standing before God. It refers to her worth, her delicacy, and her built-in sensitivity. Because of these gifts, which are unique to your wife, the admonition to you is to be careful. Gentle. Thoughtful. This can be illustrated by the way you would recklessly play touch football with your buddies in an open field compared to how you'd play inside a china shop filled with priceless and very fragile antiques. Because you know the damage a simple incomplete pass could cause, you'd play your game very differently.

2. **Do not be harsh with [her].**[25] I was on a business trip, sitting in a breakfast diner enjoying a big bowl of "home-cooked" oatmeal. Glancing through a copy of *USA Today,* I was interrupted by the sound of a shouting man. Looking up from my paper, I caught a young man—a dad, I presumed—screaming

for all he was worth directly into his child's face. I was dumb-founded. And I wasn't the only person in the place who saw this, because the whole restaurant became instantly quiet.

Before I tell you what I was thinking, let me tell you what I *wasn't* thinking: *Wow, that kid certainly must have done something egregious to earn this punishment.* Nor did I think, *Poor dad, having to put up with lots of nonsense from his insensitive and thoughtless child. Maybe now the kid will get the message.*

Here's what I *did* think: *What on earth is the matter with that guy? He ought to be locked up for treating a child like that!*

What would it—what *does* it—look like when a husband treats his wife harshly? Even in private, away from public scrutiny, it is a very ugly thing. An indefensible thing. When a man speaks harshly to his wife, he is instantly in the wrong. Every time.

The tone of your voice has everything to do with what happens in an argument. You may have already discovered that *how* you speak to your wife is as important—as fortifying or as destructive—as *what* you say to her. Some husbands may defend themselves by saying, "I'm not being harsh; she's just too sensitive." And your excuses will be as feeble as that dad's excuses would have been in the diner.

Remember that her tenderness comes as standard equipment. She *is* going to be more aware of the pitch of your voice. It's who she is, and it's one of the reasons God gave her to you. She is your ideal partner.

Fire Safety Strategy #4: When God Whispers in Your Wife's Ear, Don't Miss the Message

This strapping, exceptionally good-looking husband strolls into his million-dollar home at 8:00 every night. He gets home at this time every night because he has an every-day appointment with Leonard, his bartender. "I'd be home earlier," he says to his wife, "but my job is so stressful that, without a little liquid attitude adjustment, well, I'd be impossible to live with."

When he strides through the door, he expects—and receives—a brilliantly prepared gourmet meal. The kids, who finished dinner an hour ago, had better be quiet and well behaved. If one of them is watching *his* big-screen TV, Dad sends him scampering to a set in another room so he can download another sporting event via his satellite dish.

He has nothing but disdain for his wife's parenting methods, claiming that the children's misbehavior *must* be her fault—since he's never home. He second-guesses her every move. She lives in constant fear. And he lives with mortal unhappiness.

"Early in our marriage," she confesses, "I wanted to tell him the truth about how he made me feel. In fact, I know this is *exactly* how his father treated his mother—and him, too. He's just doing what he learned when *he* was a boy."

Although this woman has been married for almost twenty years, she tries to communicate in tender ways with her husband. Tough talk isn't an option; she's far too frightened for that. Her closest friends have heard her loving suggestions and her gentle pleas to her husband. And the man's inability—unwillingness, really—to listen to the whispers of his wife only adds to his losses. Not listening to his wife when they were first married will eventually lead to his ruin—and hers—one way or another.

When you read the biographies of great men, you'll discover—almost without exception—the strength and wisdom of their wives. These women provided far more than life-long companionship and progeny for these men. They became wise counselors, advisers, and advocates. Some received credit for the efforts from the public, but most weren't recognized for their enormous contribution until they and their prominent husbands were gone.

Early in your marriage, there's no one in the history of your life who wants to see you succeed more than your wife does. As you build this relationship into a great marriage, you're going to face disagreements and even an occasional fight. These are inevitable. But know this: The same fire that sends danger across the tall, dry grass in an open field can be used to purify precious metals. As you learn to fight fairly and to never stop listening, these brushfires with your wife just may be the very things God uses to shape your 51 percent of a terrific marriage.

9

MONEY: CROUCHING TIGER, HIDDEN CRISIS

If a husband and wife are not communicating about finances, I'll guarantee you that they're not communicating about anything.

LARRY BURKETT, FINANCIAL COUNSELOR

S ometimes the Discovery Channel is the only thing worth watching on television. Having drawn that conclusion, Bobbie and I tuned in recently to a feature called *Big Cats at Home.* It seems that there are folks scattered across the country who have a great affection for big cats—especially lions and tigers. And these people have brought these huge felines into their homes, treating them like normal house pets. The footage of these youthful animals was delightful. Cute, playful, and harmless-looking "kittens" romped on living room floors with their owners.

Eventually, however, these babies grew up. "Cute, playful, and harmless-looking" no longer served to describe them. Gliding back and forth behind backyard fences may be a beautiful sight on television, but the size of their claws, the glistening of their teeth, and the mystery of their disposition would change your perspective if you happened to live next door. Fearful neighbors have tried to force owners to get rid of their cats, but, amazingly, there's no federal law that prohibits people from raising a lion or tiger at home. (On the show, we saw some of these "house cats" that weighed over five hundred pounds! Nice kitty.)

Of course, the feature also included some pretty gruesome tales about these cats—especially the tigers—who, without provocation or warning, had attacked their neighbors or even turned on their keepers. The Discovery Channel treated us to some awful before-and-after photographs of people who had been victimized. Several had been killed.

The show's producers drew the following uncompromising conclusion: If you choose to own a tiger—or any other big cat—treat it with the utmost respect. And keep it caged at all times. Remember that a tiger can, without notice, attack—and when it does, you *will* get hurt.

CAUTION: MONEY—PROCEED AT YOUR OWN RISK

Tigers and money have a lot in common. They are both very beautiful. People stop and gawk at what they can do—jumping through fiery hoops at the circus or picking up the tab for the newest German sports sedan. They are both extremely alluring, but they can both be very dangerous if not caged properly.

And one of the reasons a book about the first year of your marriage must discuss the wonder and danger of money is that there is a good chance that you and your bride have quite different views about it:[26]

- "I'll bet that cat could run down a deer and smoke it in a split second."
- "He's so cute. Here kitty, kitty."

You may think you'll be able to tame this tiger. Trust me: it'll never happen. Your job in this first year is not to domesticate this big cat called *Money* but to cage it. And a tiger's always easier to cage before it gets big enough to do some serious damage.

Once the tiger's caged, you and your bride can spend the rest of your marriage safely enjoying its beauty and its power.

MONEY'S FALSE PROMISE

The attraction of money, of course, is what we believe it can do for us. It's why people board tour buses to view the estates of the rich and famous. Audible oohs and aahs can be heard at every turn. "Will you look at the *size* of that place!" someone will exclaim.

"Did you see all the cars in his driveway?" another will say.

I wonder what these people say about their humble little bungalows after driving back home in their twelve-year-old cars. "If only we could drive a new car and live in a house like some of those we saw on the tour," they're bound to say. "If we could have *those* things, then we'd be happy."

These same "tourists" stand in grocery store checkout lines every week. While they wait they scan the covers of their favorite weekly magazines. Every time they do, they see photographs of these same "rich and famous" people looking quite sad and pitiful. The headlines tell of "separations" and "settlements," "rehabs" and "bouts of depression." They shout about "abuse" and "estrangement." He gets the airplane; she gets the Montana ranch. He gets the cars; she gets the jewels. We're not sure who gets the children.

Maybe happy, maybe not.

Early in our marriage, our pastor, Richard Freeman, was preaching one Sunday morning about money. He was leading up to the fall "stewardship campaign," when the congregation would be asked to "subscribe to the annual budget." Everyone had their seat belts fastened.

But Rev. Freeman surprised us that morning with a truth now seared into my brain forever. "I know where to go to find a list of the most important things in your life," he announced confidently. "You've already written it down."

I was fascinated with this thought. *Prove it,* I'm sure I said to myself.

Then Rev. Freeman pulled something out of his pocket. It was his personal checkbook. Turning to the check register, he opened it and held it up. "I know where your priorities are," he said, "because here's a list of Lois Marie's and mine."

I had never thought of it like that, and I knew he was right. The way we spend our money *does* show where our priorities lie.

NORMAL . . . AGAIN

In chapter 4 we talked about family systems — about what you and your bride grew up believing was normal. Any discussion about money needs to deal with this, too. If your parents argued about money, that was normal for you. If your dad paid the household bills because he didn't trust your mother with the checkbook, that was normal. If your dad "surprised" your mother with new cars; if your mother went shopping like it was a daily sport, even when she didn't need anything; if your parents lived with heavy credit card debt; if your parents tried to hide their expenditures from each other; if your parents always waited until they could pay cash before they bought something — all of these things were normal for you. You're bringing them into your marriage as standard equipment.

CROUCHING TIGER

The other reason we're talking about money is that if you ask couples before they're married if they think money will be a big problem, most will say no. They might as well be saying, "We're not worried about money. We'll be livin' on love." And because this tiger has, so far, never done much damage to the couple, the typical bride and groom do very little about him. Through their courtship, their engagement, their wedding ceremony, and their honeymoon, the tiger sleeps. No cage necessary.

But a few months into the marriage the kitty wakes up, and things begin to change. Dramatically.

- "The sofa that Grandma gave us is heinous. We *need* a new one."
- "A golf membership would make it so much easier to take my clients out. We *need* one."
- "I've let my wardrobe deteriorate. I *need* new clothes for my job."
- "I'm tired of cooking. Let's go out again."
- "Hey, would you look at that? No money down—zero percent interest!"

In order for you to cage your tiger before it gets too unruly during this first year, here are a few "Caging Habits" that have helped many couples who want to do the right thing with their money but aren't quite sure how.

Caging Truth #1: Make a Budget and Live within Your Means

I'll never forget the first personal financial seminar I attended as a young man. The leader was a man named Ron

Blue. His clients included some of my favorite professional athletes, as well as several prominent Christian leaders.

Ron walked to the microphone, thanked his host, and greeted us. "Do you want to know the secret of financial success?" he asked. Then he answered his own question.

"You'll find financial success if you make more money than you spend and do it for a long period of time."

A couple of the students chuckled, but Ron didn't smile. Instead, he went on to explain that financial *trouble* begins when people spend more money than they have.

"It happens all the time," he said. "It happens to good people—good people like you and me, people who are unwilling to live within their means."

A few hundred years ago, spending *more* than you had would have been impossible. Can you imagine a pioneer slapping his MasterCard down to buy a horse on credit? But every time you receive your credit card bill, it tells you what your "credit limit" is. "Come on," it seems to be begging you. "Think about the good things you could buy with this *unspent* money. Go ahead. Why wait?"

Spending the money you don't have breaks Ron Blue's simple rule. Its consequence is the prevention of financial success.

The easiest way for you to stay within your means is to put a budget together—*together*. I wish Bobbie and I had done this in our early years. Once we started creating a budget together, our frustrations and arguments about money were exponentially reduced. What's more, creating a budget together gave us mutual accountability. Over the years, I have observed that a man who refuses to be accountable to his wife on financial matters is often a man who avoids accountability—of any kind—to anyone else. The beauty of accountability *to a budget* is that, at least in some sense, when you allow your budget to determine your spending decisions, you avoid being pitted against each other. In effect, you let the budget be your referee.

If you need help in creating a budget (or what may be called a spending plan), there are some terrific software programs you can buy to get you and keep you going as you manage it, month by month.[27]

Caging Truth #2: Remember That Your Wife Has Valuable Insights about Money

It was clear from the attitude of this soon-to-be husband that he had already gotten off track. He was about to marry a brilliant, talented, wealthy, recent Ivy-League college graduate, but it was clear as he and his bride sat in the premarital counselor's office that he intended to call the financial shots at home. He spoke to her in a tone dangerously close to that of an unhappy father scolding his child. As he explained his financial plans, he punctuated his points with words that made the counselor cringe.

- "She just needs to understand a few things when it comes to money."
- "I'll give her an allowance each month. When it's gone, it's gone."
- "After we get married, she's not going to be allowed to just blow money like she does now. We've already talked about this—and she understands."

It never occurred to this young man that his bride had a perspective and wisdom about money that needed to be valued. It never occurred to him that his words were thinly veiled attempts at controlling his bride. And it never occurred to him that this thoughtless control would eventually drive her away—maybe to a new mailing address without him.

There are few places where young husbands make more mistakes than when they're dealing with money. Here's a good rule to remember: If you speak to your wife about money as though she were a child, then she will believe that your concern over money is more important to you than your love for her.

Early in our marriage, Bobbie and I found ourselves embroiled in deep conflict over money. I was working on a youth worker's salary, and she had grown up in a home where money was quite freely spent.

"We can't afford that," was something I said all the time.

It wasn't that Bobbie was intentionally fighting against me; it was that she really couldn't understand our financial situation. So we decided that she would take over the checkbook. Instead of putting myself in the position of telling her what we could and couldn't afford, she could see it for herself.

This decision was a great one. Bobbie became so adept that now she was watching *my* expenses like a hawk. Our biggest first-year fight—by a long shot—was when I bought a James Taylor cassette without asking her permission. Talk about taking the ball and running with it!

Caging Truth #3: Be Careful about Taking Money from Your Parents

The chances are good that both sets of your parents have more money than you do. And it's probable that they really love you and want the best for you. So it stands to reason that there will be times when your parents are willing—whether or not you ask them—to loan you money.

Be careful.

Here's what I mean. Let's imagine that you have a circle of very close friends. And we'll imagine that one of these friends—let's call him Harold—is a loan officer at the bank. You and Harold always have a great time together. You're always relaxed when he's around, and he seems to feel the same way about you.

One day you decide to buy a new car, and because you don't have enough cash, you call your good friend, Harold. A few hours later you drive to the bank to pick up the check. Harold's waiting for you in his office and hands you the check as you walk in. You know that Harold is more than happy to loan you the money, and you have every intention of making good on the loan. However, the moment after you sign the papers and the check passes from his hand to yours, you feel something strange. It takes you a few weeks to figure out the feeling, but the next time you're with him it hits you: *Harold used to be my good friend. There was nothing between us except the fun of being in each other's presence. But now I'm a debtor to Harold. He holds a note with my name on it, and I'm obligated to him.*

Whether you like it or not, your relationship with Harold has changed—maybe until the loan is paid off. Maybe forever. You used to be friends, pure and simple. Now you're his debtor. King Solomon of ancient Israel said it well: "The rich rule over the poor, and the borrower is servant to the lender."[28]

Building a strong, unencumbered relationship with your bride's parents is an important—and sometimes challenging—goal to set. And your bride wants the same with your parents. Now it's *possible* to borrow money from them and not have it affect your relationship. It's *possible* that changing your status from son-in-law to debtor won't change anything at all. But it probably will.

If you choose to borrow from them—as a last resort—put together a payment plan in writing and stay on top of it. Pay it off early if you can. Talk about it openly when you're together. If you don't, this indebtedness can spoil (literally) your relationship.

There's one more thing about your parents' money. If they offer to *give* you money, caution is also a good idea. I have a very close friend who received a check from his wife's mother for Christmas. "Your dad and I want you to put this toward a new color television," the note inside the envelope read.

This was back in the early 1970s when color sets went for about five hundred dollars. But the check was for only a hundred dollars. That meant that this Christmas present was going to *cost* my friend four hundred dollars! And if you think he was going to be comfortable *not* having a color television the next time they visited, you'd be wrong. Some gift, huh?

Ron Blue has a wise perspective about the issue of parents giving gifts to their married children. The gift, he notes, should not obligate the couple to something they cannot afford. "Don't give them *lifestyle* money," he says. In other words, don't let your parents give you money that forces you into a lifestyle you can't afford or sustain. A hundred-dollar check toward a five-hundred-dollar color television is a perfect example; another is the down payment on an expensive home you'd have trouble maintaining.

Ron and his wife, Judy, have given their married children things like appliances. (Who *doesn't* need a good washer and dryer?) He advises parents to help their married children by sending money to pay down the principal on their mortgage or to start a savings account for their children's education. All of these are good ideas.

Caging Truth #4: Treat Your Bride Like Your Business Partner

Whether or not your wife assumes the check-writing duties, this fact is certain: Not only will you be honoring her by including her in your financial strategy, you'll also be doing yourself a great favor. Her insight will be extremely valuable.

When Mike Hyatt and I started our publishing company in 1986, we mortgaged and leveraged everything we owned. It was a scary proposition to think that no longer would we be able to refer to the funds as "my money" and "Mike's money." The money was "ours."

We made all of our financial decisions together. If I had decided to step out and hire a marketing expert or invest in a new computer system without Mike's permission, I would have sent him a disturbing message: "Even though I say that you're my partner, I'm going to make these important decisions without you."

Treat your wife like your business partner. Think strategically about expenditures and investments together. Do your best not to talk about "my" money and "your" money.[29] Someday, if children come along and your wife decides to be an at-home mom, you may be *forced* to treat your money as "ours." I can't think of any good reason to wait for that day. Establish your "partnership" right away.

Caging Habit #5: Put Giving into Your Regular Budget

How I use money is a snapshot of what's truly important to me. At a single glance I can see what I value most. I may think that giving to my church or other worthy charities can wait until I have more money, but I know from experience that if Bobbie and I hadn't gotten into the habit of being generous early, it would have been impossible to do it later.

Practicing charity came to me as a gift from my parents. It was one of my *normals*. My parents were tithers—they gave away at least 10 percent of their income every year. So one of the early financial decisions Bobbie and I made was to be sure that, at the end of the year, our donations totaled at least 10 percent of our income. We didn't do this so that God would be obligated to bless us in some special way; we did it because we had learned that this was the right thing to do. And we discovered that stewardship was its *own* reward, which is exactly why the Bible says that "you're far happier giving than receiving."[30]

The donation we could barely afford in our first year became a pattern of generosity that we're both thankful for. In the end, it's easier to make strategic decisions about giving money away when you're first married and living on less than when you find yourself with more someday. It may be easier to give ten cents out of every dollar than a hundred-thousand dollars out of every million!

If you stop making mortgage payments on your house, the lender will eventually foreclose on you. If you neglect to keep up with your car payments, the bank will send a flatbed truck and winch your car away. But if you stop giving to your church or to the support of missionaries, they'll suffer quietly.

Holding your money with an open hand will be a reminder to you that it's a gift in the first place. It's why your church typically labels its fund drive as *stewardship*. A steward never "owns" anything. Instead, he is charged with taking care of someone else's property. Your open hand will remind you that money is a blessing to be shared rather than an asset to be hoarded.

Besides, closing your hand will spill lots of it.

Caging Truth #6: Set a "Fun Money" Spending Limit

I was on the phone with a businessman I really respect. He runs a large division of a 150-year-old multinational corporation, and he runs it very successfully. My friend loves his work, and he reminds me of this every time we talk.

Somewhere in our conversation he mentioned his spending limit. We had been talking about an investment that I thought would be a good idea for his division. "I'll have to talk to the CEO," he said. "A hundred-thousand dollars is above my spending limit."

My friend is happy in his work, because within this "spending limit" he has the freedom to make choices. His entrepreneurial instincts—exercised inside these boundaries—make his work inspiring and motivating.

Early in your marriage, you and your bride should set a no-permission-necessary spending limit. It may be ten dollars, a hundred dollars, or more. Also, you may want to set a "frequency limit"—once a week, twice a month, or whatever is agreeable to both of you. This money will give you both a sense of freedom without jeopardizing your budget. When you're out and you see something that falls within your agreed-on limits, you can go for it.

Mark and Susan advise newlyweds to adopt a similar approach. They call it the *Marriage Insurance Premium* (MIP)—a certain amount of money set aside each month for you to spend without your spouse's permission. Having a MIP creates an expanse of freedom for each of you, a space in which you can make small financial decisions in ways that fit your style and personality. Without it, you and your wife could easily feel constricted and trapped.

Caging Truth #7: Pursue Contentment

Early in our marriage, if someone had told me that making a lot more money would not make me happy, I would have laughed out loud. Of course, I was familiar with the cliché about money and happiness, but I *knew* it was foolish and doubtful.

Down through the years of our life together, however, Bobbie and I have watched some of our friends gather wealth. In some cases, fabulous wealth. And we've made many acquaintances with "people of means." In some cases, fabulous means. And we've made the following observation—one that has, so far, yielded no exceptions: If these people were happy before they got wealthy, they still seemed to be happy. And if these people were not happy before their ships came in, money didn't change this situation either.

When I was twenty years old, I—along with thirty-nine friends—crossed the United States on a bicycle. There were, however, three ten-thousand-foot passes lurking between the Pacific and the Atlantic Oceans. One thing I remember about climbing the western slopes of these behemoths was that, as we rounded bends in the road—thinking we were at the top—there were still *more* hills to climb. Getting to the very top felt like an endless assignment.

Spending your way to happiness will never happen. When you *finally* buy that thing "you've always wanted," your little bicycle will round the bend in the road, and voilà, there's another "if only I could have that" waiting for you. You'll never reach the top of this mountain.

So what should you do? Take a deep breath, and realize that your climb for acquiring things looks more like a hamster's wheel than a goal you can achieve. You're far more likely to spin than win. Understanding this fact—and believing its truth—will begin to help you on your journey toward contentment.

Caging Truth #8: Money Is a Neutral Substance

You can go into a bookstore and find books about money that claim to be written from a Christian perspective. Some of these books will tell you that money—especially having a lot of it—is a very bad thing; on the other hand, you'll be able to find titles telling you that having lots of money is God's way of rewarding you for your obedience. Can you imagine such opposite positions—both of which purport to represent a Christian perspective?

Here's where we're coming from. We think it cuts to the heart of the issue: "The love of money is a root of all kinds of evil. Some people, eager for money, have wandered from the faith and pierced themselves with many griefs."[31]

Water is a neutral substance. It can be a thirst-quenching lifesaver after a basketball game or a jog through the neighborhood. But a person can also drown in water. A baseball bat is also a neutral substance. A slugger can use it to park a line drive over the centerfield fence and win the game for his team, or a thug can use it to kill an innocent victim.

Money is a neutral substance. It can be used for good things, or it can lead to a person's demise. The variable isn't the money itself but the way in which it's treated. The non-negotiables about money are these:

- Don't fall in love with it; use it—but use it wisely.
- Don't spend more than you have—except for a reasonable mortgage, stay out of debt.
- Share financial decisions with your wife.

- Give away as much of it as you can.

Out of respect for what it can do—both good and bad—hold your money, however much you have, with an open hand. This *restrained* tiger is a beautiful thing.

10

SEX: BATTER UP

There are three things that are too amazing
for me,
    four that I do not understand.
the way of an eagle in the sky,
    the way of a snake on a rock,
the way of a ship on the high seas,
    and the way of a man with a maiden.

PROVERBS 30:18–19

———◆•✦•◆———

I want both of you to close your eyes and think of as many sexual fantasies about each other that you can."

Though Mark and Susan have done premarital counseling with more couples than they can remember, they'll never forget being asked this question in their own premarital preparation. The question was not a complete surprise, since the minister who asked the question trafficked in the unexpected. This was a man who had an uncanny ability to bring Jesus into the most unlikely places in the most unexpected ways.

"I'll give you sixty seconds," the minister said.

Mark, happy to obey his pastor, closed his eyes and started thinking. What Susan was going to do with the question wasn't his immediate concern.

"Time's up!" the minister announced with a flourish. Mark looked straight at him, feeling a little squeamish about what he had just done while sitting in church—in the pastor's office!

"Now let me tell you what just happened," the minister began, releasing Mark from having to describe what had just galloped through this mind.

Pointing to Mark, the minister continued, "This young man just thought of twenty or thirty different possibilities. But his bride-to-be is still trying to think of the first one." Mark glanced in Susan's direction. Her blush and shy giggle communicated the pastor's accuracy.

At that moment, Mark realized what you and I already now know. The anatomical differences between husbands and wives don't compare to the immense differences in the places we'll never see—our brains and our hearts.

MEET MR. CLUELESS

Years later, Mark found himself seated across from a young couple just three months into their marriage. Because of scheduling snafus, the couple was only able to complete four of the five premarital sessions before the wedding. So the fifth and final meeting was now taking place a few months *after* the wedding.

In this session, Mark typically discusses the process (and power) of building a mutually satisfying sex life. "Men have a tendency to misunderstand their wives' needs when it comes to sex," Mark said. "They often assume that, because they are satisfied, their wives must be satisfied as well."

As he talked, the bride nodded in agreement. She knew exactly what Mark was saying. The groom, on the other hand, was becoming less and less attentive, his eyes scanning the family photographs on Mark's desk and the Bible commentaries in the bookcase.

The wife had had enough. "Are you getting this?" she asked, just enough edge in her voice to let her husband know that she wasn't pleased with his attitude.

"Come on, honey," the young man replied, a distinct dash of bravado in his voice. "Do you *really* think we need help in this area?" His eyes moved from his bride to Mark, and the swagger in his countenance intensified. His next words confirmed that here was a man in the process of being made utterly stupid by his own virility. "I'd say we've pretty much got this part down."

The young bride sat up straight in her chair and looked directly into her husband's face. "You've definitely figured out how to make *yourself* happy, big guy," she snapped, "but you've still got a thing or two to learn about me."

The silence that followed was poignant and intentional. Mark wanted to let the wife's words soak deeply into her husband's mind. The flush of his face revealed that her pointed remark had made a direct hit.

TAKE ME OUT TO THE BALL GAME

Let's face it, intercourse is intercourse. Making our body parts fit together is not terribly complicated. "No assembly required" may as well be printed on our marriage licenses. But for your wife, this isn't enough—not even close to enough. Making the emotional and physical connections in ways that are completely satisfying to her is a whole different . . . ball game.

From the time we were youngsters—sixth grade rings a bell—we and our buddies started talking about "running the bases." And I'm not talking about baseball. You remember hearing guys joke about getting to first base with a girl—then second base, and so on? I don't recall anyone ever putting specific definitions to these markers, but I think we assumed that holding hands and kissing were included in running out a single. French kissing may have described the dash from first to second, but above-the-waist petting definitely announced your arrival there. Hitting third base meant full-body petting—anything short of intercourse. And, of course, home plate was the ultimate.

Do you remember what each of these felt like the first time you experienced them? For most men, regardless of their age or lifelong sexual exploits, these "firsts" were unforgettable. I've noticed some interesting things about the way most boys talk about these bases during their adolescence.

Unforgettable First Arrivals

The *first time* is an incredible experience—even first base.

Because my dad was a minister, sitting in church was as common to our family as sitting at the kitchen table. So, of course, my first encounters with nonfamily girls were at church. Anything remotely resembling "social interaction" in grade school is a total blur, but church was different. I remember noticing girls during my adolescent Sunday school years, primarily because they always sat with each other and had terminal cases of the giggles.

I was sitting next to her in church the first time I made contact with a girl's hand. We both had our arms folded across our chests, which allowed our inside hands to reach out and touch. They did. My heart raced. I'm sure my ears turned bright red. My entire body tingled. I felt like Kirk Gibson in the first game of the 1988 World Series. The pastor may have been waxing his most brilliant eloquence, but I was completely missing it.

This was incredible. I was alive.

Base Fatigue

I coached my first Little League team in the fall of 2000. I learned that, even for youngsters, getting to first base may be a thrill but who wants to stay there? Dancing the jig a few feet toward second is an art form. Of course, the purpose is to entice a pickoff attempt from the pitcher in the hope that the throw would be wild so they could scamper down to second.

It's quite a simple thing. Once you get to a base, your interest isn't in staying there but in moving on. Staying on the same base for any length of time at all is—well, it's a little boring.

Baserunning Experience

Once you've spent time at first base, the next time you run the bases you hustle past it on your way to second. Been there, done that.

When our daughters turned sixteen, they had our permission to "single-date"—out for the evening with one boy. Young men were aware of our "dating rule at age sixteen," so as we approached the girls' birthdays, Bobbie and I couldn't help but notice the boys circling the field.

We had another rule in addition to the minimum age limit. Boys who were interested in taking our girls out had to be interviewed by me.[32] Our second daughter's first date was going to be with an older boy. He was eighteen. During the interview I asked Steven if he had had a long-term dating relationship before.

"Yes, sir," he said.

"How long did you date her?" I asked.

"Oh, about a year," was his reply.

Because this was Julie's very first dating experience and because Steven was something of a veteran, I gently warned him about his baserunning speed. "Don't assume," I said— beads of perspiration were forming along his temples as I spoke— "that you can quickly move to where you've been with another girl. This is Julie's first experience."

"Yes, sir," he said again, his lips turning purple from oxygen deprivation.

LEARNING TO TALK ABOUT SEX

Several years ago, an older couple walked into Mark's office. What the husband said in the first few minutes would have been laughable if it hadn't been so tragic. "It's been years—maybe ten—since my wife and I have had any sort of physical intimacy," he confessed. "It's gotten so bad I've decided we needed some counseling."

Marriage disintegration usually begins in secret places—places no one else can see, places husbands and wives avoid. And sexual intimacy is one of the most frequently circumvented subjects. Many couples learn the magic of open dialogue about every dimension of their lives together—every dimension, that is, except sex. And because of this neglect, sex often becomes an area of simmering frustration and tangible defeat.

Early in your marriage, you need to learn to express your needs clearly, and your wife needs to do the same. And I'm not talking about sarcastic comments during sex. "Can I get you something to *read*?" doesn't qualify as productive sex talk.

"I really want to make love to you tonight," a husband needs to feel free to say kindly to his wife over breakfast.

"When you do that to me, it drives me wild," a wife must be able to say without inhibition.

When we mention the need for this kind of openness— especially to unmarried, engaged men—we're often met with a verbal (or nonverbal), "I could NEVER say that!" Then we remind them of the Old Testament's challenge to concentrate our efforts for the *whole first year* on learning to bring pleasure to our wives. And how can a husband possibly learn to please his wife without talking about what pleases her?

To get to the answer, we begin once again with our family of origin—our *normals.* If your parents showed no physical affection in your presence, that was a *normal.* If you never saw them touching each other tenderly, you may have been convinced that your parents found you under a lily pad, because they *never* would have done THAT to bring you into their family!

If your parents talked about how dirty and awful sex was, that was a *normal.* If your parents walked around the house in their underwear (or less); if you saw your parents flirt with other adults in public but not with each other; if you never heard a single word of advice about sex when you were small; and if you were (and are still) certain that your mother is incapable of saying the word *intercourse*—all of these things were normal for you.

Your challenge is to recognize your sexual *normal,* and either celebrate it because it was so healthy or learn from it because it wasn't. Then you can begin to feel free to talk about it with your wife. Chances are better than 50/50 that she's eager to talk with you.

Out of the Base Path and onto the Playground

Learning about sex in baseball terms probably got us off track back there in sixth grade. In baseball you "slam, slide, dive, hit, smash, drive, blast—and win." So you've concluded now that sex is something you *do.* You step up to the plate, or you wind up and deliver. You do something *to* someone.

Perhaps we'd be in a much better place if we had used the

playground as our sexual image instead. Here's what a playground provides that baseball misses completely.

Variety

I'm sure you've never seen a playground that has only one kind of structure to play on. Can you imagine how silly it would be to drive past a school and see a dozen seesaws and nothing else—or only swing sets or only jungle gyms?

Baseball has rules—hundred of rules. Just because a player decides it'd be more fun to run on a fly ball than tag up, it doesn't change the rule. Three strikes is an "out" every time. There is no room for flexibility at all. In fact, some free spirits wonder why they call it a "game."

The fun of the playground is the pleasure of variety. When it comes to sex with your wife, treat the experience as though you're on the playground, not between a couple of chalk lines. Changing settings, times of the day, positions, and locations are all perfectly legal. You will not be charged with an error on account of your creativity. Of course, because it's play, be sure that your playmate is having fun, too. This is profoundly important to keep in mind.

Spontaneity

I really don't know why they do this, but baseball games almost always start at fixed times—strange times like 1:05 P.M. or 7:20 P.M. And at the beginning of each season, the players know exactly who they'll be playing and where for the next six months.

Even among individual players, strict workout regimens rule each day. A player, just because he feels like it, cannot decide to take batting practice before breakfast or lift weights during the sixth inning. There's simply no room for impulsiveness or spontaneity.

But your intimacy with your wife is very different from baseball. It is not something that has to be regularly scheduled. It's neither your right to make unyielding demands with regard to frequency nor her privilege to go on strike.

Laughter

There's almost nothing funny about a baseball game. You hear cheers, boos, shouts, insults, and calls for the umpires' heads. There's very little laughter, unless the humor is directed at a player's unplanned blooper. But if you roll your windows down near a busy neighborhood playground, you're going to hear squeals of delight and laughter.

One of the most visible indicators of a healthy marriage is the ability to laugh. Watching silly movies and sharing jokes between you and your wife are just as important as spine-tingling sex. Some women would say, in fact, that one leads to the other.

Mark and I have a mutual Christian friend who is a sex therapist. She says, "There are 150 positions for intercourse, and only two of them can be successfully accomplished without laughing."

Everybody Wins

Can you imagine a child complaining to his mother that he "lost at the swing set" or that he "was defeated at the merry-go-round"? The beauty of the playground is that *play* is the goal. In order for there to be success, one group doesn't need to grind another group's nose in nasty defeat. Because play is the only goal, both sides win.

"Tonight I'm at your complete service," a husband may say to his wife before bed. "Your wish is my command—anything you want will be my pleasure." Call this guy a "loser" in baseball, but in lovemaking he captures the Cy Young award, the batting crown, and the Most Valuable Player award in a single night.

Of course, his award ceremony is celebrated a few nights later when his wife makes the same unconditional offer to him. I think we've just defined a win-win.[33]

MISSION POSSIBLE: LEARNING YOUR WIFE'S SECRETS TO GREAT SEX

There are different kinds of thrilling moments in baseball. Certainly the clutch home run is a biggie—like Kirk Gibson's in 1988. The no-hitter and the triple play are amazing and extremely rare. But one of my favorite baseball delights is the inside-the-park home run. In fact, with the reduced size of many of the new ballparks, these are becoming more and more infrequent.

Even if you're not a big baseball fan, you probably already know that when a player hits a ball into one of the outfield gaps and legs out a home run, he *must* touch all the bases. If he doesn't, the opposing team can contest it—and he can be called "out."

Okay, so you knew this. But did you know that even if a batter clears the fence with a dinger, he *still* has to touch all the bases or his home run doesn't count as a home run? Robin Ventura was reminded of this rule in the 1999 National League Championship Series against Atlanta, when he hit a towering extra-inning home run into the right-centerfield bleachers with the bases loaded. His teammates ran from the dugout and mobbed him as he rounded first. The game was over, and the Mets had won. But because Robin never made it around the bases, he was credited with a "grand-slam single."

Now that you're married and "getting to home plate" is normal fare, you may be tempted to take an immediate left turn out of the batter's box, simply dashing to third base and back. In fact, you may even be tempted to stay right there at home plate. Hey, every at bat is a winner. Right?

Well, actually, no. And this is exactly what the young bride was trying to tell her groom in Mark's office that day. If her husband doesn't remember his baserunning skills and practice them regularly, she'll lose interest in no time at all.

For a man, the thrill of sex is the destination. But for his wife, it's all about the journey. As far as she's concerned—even though she's married and "scoring" is a given—if he doesn't touch all her bases, his home run doesn't count.

So what are some of your wife's secrets to great sex? What does it mean to "touch all the bases"? If you have the companion book, *What Every Bride Needs to Know*, turn to page 137. Read what a woman thinks this "baseball game" should look like.

Touching

Do you remember the life-size wall chart in biology class that showed the human nervous system? Coming out from the guy's brain were lines that looked like rivers and tributaries, branching out again and again until they covered his whole body.

Try to remember where you saw the greatest collection—the highest concentration—of nerve endings. A chapter on sex may send you to the wrong place, because the answer is—your fingertips.

There are no words to describe the power of touch, especially to a woman. It's almost as though there's a nerve that runs straight from her fingertips to her heart.

Many husbands fall into the pattern of never touching their wives except in a sexual context. And these men wonder why their brides are less than enthusiastic about those touches. The truth is that the places she wants to be touched often don't even show up on our baselines. Some days she may want you to brush her hair. Another day she may need a neck massage. On a different day the biggest turn-on for her may be having her feet rubbed. If the only sexual game you know is baseball, you will likely strike out.

So when you're sitting next to her at a concert or riding along in the car, reach over and hold her hand. When you're striding from your parking spot at the mall, take her hand. When you sit across from her in a restaurant and you're waiting for your food, take her hand while you talk together. You probably did these things when you were dating her—and there's no good reason to stop now!

Kissing

I'm no expert on rules that prostitutes follow, but there is one that's universally known. When they're with a client, there's absolutely nothing that's unacceptable—out-of-bounds. Every conceivable position or fantasy the client may have is fair game. It's what he's paying for. However, kissing is strongly discouraged. This act communicates a love and an intimacy that even the most bizarre forms of sex cannot match. Don't you find that amazing?

Too many couples stop kissing once they get married. Even though you've only been married for a short time, perhaps you've noticed this yourself.

I married a woman who loves to kiss. It makes me tired just thinking about it, but when we were engaged, we could literally— I'm not making this up—kiss, *just* kiss, for hours. Sometimes we'd stop (I'd be taking gulps of air) and talk about how much fun it will be when we're married.

"We can kiss all night long," Bobbie would say.

It wasn't exactly what I had in mind, but I let her run with the thought.

The next time you're making love, stop what you're doing and give your wife a deep, long, passionate kiss. Give her an exact replica of the one you gave her when you asked her to marry you. See if I'm right about this kissing thing.

Talking

Here we go again—talking about talking. But here I'm not talking about free and open conversations about the *subject* of sex. I'm not referring to candid "what gives me pleasure" talks or "I need us to make love tonight" comments.

No, this kind of talk is as important to a woman as any kind of foreplay could be. It's tender talk, affirming words, the kind of gentle things you spoke when you were trying to win her heart in the first place. These are sounds she needs to hear again in a setting that's quiet and conducive to soft conversation:

- "I love the way you smile."
- "I'm the luckiest guy on the planet because of you."
- "You have the most beautiful eyes I've ever seen."

Ordinarily your lives are filled with "task talk":

- "Could you pick up the dry cleaning?"
- "What time is dinner?"
- "Have you seen my Palm Pilot?"

- "Hey, it's Thursday. Would you mind taking out the trash?"

The tender words I have in mind, however, have no destination but her heart. No goal to achieve, but simply to remind her that if you had it to do all over again, you would.

All these things—touching, kissing, and talking (and maybe a few more you and your wife can discover together)—will guarantee home runs that show up in the record books.

PRESSURE AND REJECTION: TURNING OFF THE SPIN CYCLE

The most common—and destructive—pattern a couple can experience is the unnecessary cycle of pressure and rejection. If it hasn't happened to you yet, it will.

There will be times when one of you is particularly interested in lovemaking at the very time the other seems to be indifferent. As a result, the pursued partner feels pressured, and the pursuing partner feels rejected. This is not an amusing scene at all. Left unaddressed, this situation can degenerate into a seething resentment that can spread poison throughout your whole relationship.

Though this pattern isn't the least bit surprising, what is remarkable is how few couples *ever* discuss it, much less work out possible scenarios to ameliorate the situation. Many couples simply cross their fingers and hope things work out on their own. It's a strategy that can set you up for a lifetime of frustration.

And, in spite of the stereotype of the pursuer and pursued, it's not always the man who is the aggressor. (Does it surprise you that the most popular sexual stimulant in history—Viagra—is a product for *men?*)

Here are a couple ideas that may be helpful. If they sound like kid stuff, it may be because they're nothing more than guidelines—*rules* are for baseball, remember? These may help you and your bride enjoy sexual play without wounding each other's heart. Though none of the following ideas are perfect, they are sure to work better than the common "gee-whiz, I sure hope this works out, knock on wood" approach that many couples fall into.

The "Almost Never Say No" Ideal

Because most couples will agree that sex is almost *always* a good idea, here's your sexual default: "If you're really in the mood, I can get there." And face it, you'll most likely look back on what you've just experienced, and, regardless of who was up for it and who wasn't, you'll both admit that it really *was* a good idea.

Right now, early in your marriage, you may want to adopt this "almost never say no" policy. No, it's not an unbreakable rule. It's just that you'll decide that it will always be your priority to *try* to meet your spouse's needs.

The spirit of this default is not unlike what happens when your wife says to you, "Hey, I'd love to go out for a walk tonight." Even though you may not be in a walking mood, you take a deep breath and lace up your walking shoes. You may give a qualified yes by saying, "I'd love to walk with you, but if it's okay, let's just go around the block once. I'm exhausted." In the same way, the spouse invited into unscheduled lovemaking may say, "Actually, I don't think I'm up for thirty minutes of WWF main event, but if you're up for something quick, sign me up."

When you're the one doing the asking, it may be wise to remember that your bride's response to this encounter may not make her an Academy Award finalist. "Way to put your heart into it, honey" after this rendezvous could put you in a difficult negotiating position later on.

Quid Pro Quo

Regardless of her best "never say no" intentions, there *are* going to be times when your bride is just not going to say yes. Because you're at the playground and not at Yankee Stadium, let it go. Believe it or not, there will be times when the shoe is on the other foot and you'll be needing a healthy dose of understanding from your wife.

Although we discourage lighted scoreboards mounted on your bedroom wall, we *do* encourage keeping informal track of your own noes and yeses. There's nothing wrong with hearing, "Hey, this didn't work into my plan the other night, and even though I'm still not feeling like Cleopatra—sure, let's."

What's important in these "not tonight, honey" moments is that the rejection of the act of lovemaking doesn't mean that you or your wife have suddenly contracted terminal leprosy. Your or your wife's no to making love didn't mean anything but simply that. Nothing more.

If you're on the receiving end of the no, don't take it personally. If you're doing the rejecting, a little tenderness accompanying the "no, thanks" will go a long way.

In addition to these two guidelines, you and your wife may come up with some playground principles of your own. We know a couple who does "rock, paper, scissors" when they can't agree. And the losing spouse can always ask for "best two out of three" if he or she is *really* serious. The secret is to discuss these playground principles *before* the situation presents itself, when harmony and rational thinking are at work.

When unruffled people are engaged in problem solving, constructive ideas are usually the natural result.

MADE FOR EACH OTHER

One of the things God put into marriage and your sexual union is the mystery of *interdependence*. You begin to literally *need* each other. Let me explain.

Bobbie and I were having dinner with our daughter, Missy, and her husband, Jon. Since Missy was nursing her newborn, she had timed the outing with the baby-sitter so the baby wouldn't need to be fed before she returned. The restaurant service was quite slow, so our dinner experience took longer than we had expected. Although Missy wasn't in pain—that's easy for me to say!—she *was* beginning to get a little uncomfortable. "I'm going to need to nurse pretty soon," she said. (Did you notice she said that *she* needed to nurse?)

Just then, a baby began crying from a quiet corner of the restaurant.

"Oh, dear," Missy said, quickly lifting her dinner napkin up to cover herself. Because Missy's body was primed to nurse, the sound of a crying baby triggered her breast milk on cue, soaking the front of her dress. Jon quickly gave her his sport coat.

Isn't it amazing how God connects a mother and her baby in this way? When the baby is born, there's nothing more satisfying than the taste of his or her mother's milk. And once that process begins, a mother has just as much need to *give* her milk as her child has to *receive* it. There's interdependence at work.

The analogy ought to be obvious. When you and your wife step into marriage and begin to engage in regular lovemaking, your bodies begin to "look forward" to each other — to literally long for each other in a spirit of interdependence.

The Sobering Side of This Truth

In the story of Missy and her baby, let's imagine that her baby woke up and was crying for something to eat. Instead of waiting for the mother, the baby-sitter whipped up some baby formula and fed the child. Like magic, the baby drank a bottle of formula and went back to sleep.

Then suppose Missy walks in. "How's the baby?" she asks the sitter.

"Great. He woke up about an hour ago and started to cry. I fed him a bottle of formula, and now he's sleeping again."

This may have been fine for the baby, but his mother would have been miserable.[34] In this incredible relationship between child and mother, God gave them *both* a drive — a hunger — to be satisfied by each other.

You know where this is going, don't you? "How 'bout it?" between you and your wife is more than just a matter of enjoying a playful romp on a grassy knoll. It's more than just the fulfillment of one of those fantasies that Mark conjured up during his own premarital counseling. Sexual intercourse is literally the satisfying of a craving that God gave you for your wife. And it fulfills a hunger that she has for you, too.

The reality is this: you *need* each other sexually.

SPOILING YOUR APPETITE

It's physiologically possible for you to relieve your pent-up need for your wife *without* her — to spoil your appetite, so to speak.

Of course, infidelity does exactly this. As guilty as you'd be of stealing if you hot-wired your neighbor's new car and drove it off, you're robbing your wife of what belongs to her. Yes, your heart belongs to her. Yes, your future belongs to her. But your *body* and what it provides for her—the hunger it satisfies—also belongs to her. And because great sex includes more than just landing on home plate, any kind of baserunning activity with anyone else but your wife is a truly bad idea for at least two important reasons:

1. It robs your wife of what *belongs to her* exclusively. The damage that's done creates a lifetime scar—and in many cases it spells the beginning of the end.
2. You and your wife have become adept at lovemaking through lots of trial and error, and therefore your new experience will *not* be as good. This may come as a surprise to you, but it is almost always true.

Psychiatrist and family therapist Frank Pittman, after counseling with thousands of couples who had had extramarital affairs, concluded, "Most affairs consist of a little bad sex and lots of hours on the telephone."[35] Another study confirmed Pittman's assessment, citing real numbers: While 67 percent of men and 55 percent of women found marital sex to be very pleasurable, only 47 percent of men and 37 percent of women describe extramarital sex to be very pleasurable.[36]

But even in the face of the statistical data, many men still find themselves enmeshed in affairs. And almost 100 percent of these men fall into illicit relationships through talking and touching and kissing. (See how powerful these things are?) Some men we've talked to even reported how much more freely they were able to *pray* with their new love than with their wives. They insisted that in the early stages there was "nothing sexual" about their relationship. However, if this kind of "nonsexual" affair is not terminated, it *will* eventually lead to intercourse—remember the Little Leaguers dancing the jig away from those boring bases?

What's more, just because a man is happily married and sexually satisfied, there's no guarantee that he's not a candidate for an affair. In counseling, some men have even said, "It's only my body; I *still* love my wife"—a common excuse that has a predictable outcome. Even couples who recover from infidelity carry deep scars for the rest of their lives. Talk to someone with one of those scars. He'll tell you what I'm telling you: *It's not worth it!*

Temptation to infidelity will be a relentless adversary your whole life. So be on guard. Act like a recovering alcoholic with plenty of money, who lives across the street from a liquor store. He *could* walk across the street—he may even *want* to walk across the street, but he *knows* that "just one drink" will kill him. So he stays right where he is and hangs on to his sobriety. "One day at a time," his bumper sticker reads. Your commitment to sexual faithfulness needs to be the same. Never drop your guard because you think you're bulletproof. You aren't.[37]

Virtual Affairs

Real infidelity isn't the only way your body can be stolen from your wife. You can do it virtually. Every man can remember his first look at a pornographic image. I had mine when I was a sophomore in college. Lucky for me, there was no Internet in 1967.

Today pornography is cramming cyberspace and is as available as my toothbrush. Almost every day, I'm invited to see "hot young babes" or "hungry sluts" right here on my computer. Because my software shows me the first couple lines of a message before I download it, I'm further enticed to check out quickly what's waiting for me. Every time I see these invitations there, waiting for me, my heart jumps. My pulse goes up *every single time.*

I will always be a drunk just across the street from plenty of booze, and I know it. What I also know is that if I cave in, I will be guilty of committing grand theft. My unsuspecting wife will lose something precious because of my foolishness.

I want to. I'd like to. I'm really curious to see what's waiting for me. I take a deep breath and hit the delete key. And you must do the same. Forgive me for sounding as dogmatic as your junior high gym teacher, but there's no leeway here; there's just no middle ground. I've seen firsthand—and in the lives of close friends—what this "drug" does to a man's soul.[38] Please hit the delete key. You *must* hit your delete key. Not for me—but for your wife *and* for you. If you cave in, it'll ruin you.

Just One Look

Because I travel quite a bit, I often walk through airports. The way some of these are designed, a person can get a full aerobic workout merely transferring from one plane to another. As I walk the concourses, I see lots of interesting people. Some of these people are women, and some of them really shouldn't be wearing what they're wearing in public.

I truly have no control over taking the first glance. But I've promised myself—and my wife—that I'll not look again. When my eyes send a signal to my brain that indicates something like "really large breasts at 10 o'clock" or "tight short skirt at 3 o'clock," I *choose* not to look back.[39] It's not that I'm afraid I'll actually *do* something illicit right there in the airport. It's just that I know I'm standing at another threshold of a virtual affair. If I step across it, I will be stealing from—and dishonoring—my wife. So I don't look again.

Is it easy? No, but you'll get used to it.

ALL THE MARBLES

I love watching athletes celebrate great victories. A golfer hugging his caddie or a baseball player being mobbed at home plate after hitting a game-winning home run often brings tears to my eyes. Because my own athletic prowess never reached broadcast proportions, I cannot identify with what it means to win on such a grand scale. Or can I?

Orel Hershiser, baseball's most dominant pitcher in 1988, unanimous winner of the Cy Young award and the Most Valuable Player award for the National League Championship Series and the World Series, was asked about what it felt like—winning in front of the whole world. His response may surprise you: "Of course I was thrilled beyond words. Completely in awe. But this feeling is no different from when you make the honor roll or watch your bride walk down the aisle or hold your own child for the first time or close a big business deal. You *know* that feeling."[40]

It's true that each of these things is a thrill. However, because I know him, I know there's one more thing Orel could add to his list: *the satisfaction of fidelity*. Winning at the challenge of intimacy with your wife and overcoming the relentless temptations of infidelity will bring you an even greater satisfaction than winning the World Series or the Stanley Cup or the Masters.

Your discipline, hard work, and self-denial will have paid off—and you'll have more fun on the playground than you could have ever imagined.

11

IN-LAWS: WHO ARE THESE PEOPLE AND WHAT DO THEY WANT FROM ME?

When a man walks his daughter down the aisle and turns her over to another man, it's like handing a priceless Stradivarius violin to a gorilla.

JAY KESLER, PRESIDENT EMERITUS, TAYLOR UNIVERSITY

I'm an in-law.

I got this way by walking our two daughters — Missy in 1994 and Julie in 1999 — down the aisle at First Presbyterian Church in Nashville, Tennessee. The feeling I had during each of these very long walks was identical. Let me see if I can describe it for you:

These women came into my life in 1971 and 1974, respectively. Moments after their birth, I was presented with their pocket-size bodies. I looked into their little faces. I lifted theirs to mine and kissed their tiny rosebud mouths. Their eyes rolled back and forth, trying to focus; their miniature arms and legs flailed. The feelings in the deepest corners of my heart were wonder and overwhelming delight. "Daddy," I whispered to them. "I'm your daddy."

Now these babies were women. Their hands rested on my right forearm, and we moved along in procession to the glorious organ music that filled the sanctuary like a thick mist, penetrating every nook and crevice. I was numb from the top of my head to the bottoms of my feet.

As I walked slowly down the aisle next to these brides, I wish I could tell you that the feeling was the same rapture I felt when I gave them their first kiss in the hospital. But it wasn't. This wasn't a wedding; it was a funeral. And deep in my soul, I knew it.

IT WAS ALSO ANOTHER BIRTH

Are you shocked that I'd say something like this—comparing our daughters' weddings to a funeral? First, let me assure you—without the slightest hesitation—that the men our daughters chose to marry are incredible. Jon and Christopher are the answers to the prayers we said as Bobbie and I knelt alongside our young daughters' beds:

> *"Lord, please bless the boys that Missy and Julie will marry. Please protect them today. Help them to be obedient to their parents. And teach them to love you. Amen."*

The girls would also pray for these boys—wherever they were:

> *"Help them not to fall off their bikes and hurt themselves."*

Our prayers had been answered. We couldn't have been more thrilled with the young men who stood at the end of that long aisle. Bobbie and I loved them and were overjoyed with Missy and Julie's choices.

So my dark feeling wasn't because I disliked Jon or Christopher in any way. What I knew, however, was that this spelled the death of something—*and* the birth of something else.

Until this moment, I had been the most important man in their lives—the daddy, "the Big Kahuna." As their parents, Bobbie and I had been the go-to folks for decisions, both big and small. Our home was their home. But on this day—in one instant—all of that died.

"Who gives this woman to be married to this man?" Mark DeVries asked me. His eyes and mine were swimming in tears.

What was born in that ceremony was a new "most important" man, a new go-to guy, a new home—a brand-new marriage. And on those two wedding days something else was born—roles Bobbie and I had never known before: father-in-law and mother-in-law. Our twenty-three-year and twenty-five-year relationships with our daughters were instantly demoted to second-string. For each of them, there was a new superstar in town.

Not until these weddings did I fully realize what I had done to Bobbie's parents when I married her and moved them down a notch to the status of *in-laws*. I tell you this to help you understand why your in-laws are acting strangely. But as I said, *you're* in charge of this relationship now, even though you're the new kid on the block.

SIDE WITH YOUR WIFE

The first law of in-law relationships is this: Always side with your wife first.

Louis and Joanna had been married for less than a year when Joanna forgot her mother-in-law's birthday. I say

"*Joanna* forgot"—because both Louis and Joanna grew up in homes where the unspoken and unquestioned rule was this: the wife takes responsibility for remembering birthdays, anniversaries, and all gifts for both sides of the family.

Even so, the direct attack from her father-in-law caught her completely off guard. He called her at work, but he skipped the normal pleasantries. There was a sharpness and intensity about his anger as he spoke: "How could you forget her birthday? This year, of all years—when she's done so much for you!"

Forget the fact that Joanna's husband, Louis—the woman's own son—had forgotten this birthday as well. Forget the fact that, just three months into the marriage, there were enough adjustments for a new bride to make. This father-in-law was incensed, and he gave full vent to his anger, leveling Joanna with a stout reminder of her failure.

Hours later, when Joanna met up with Louis back at their home, she still wasn't over the trauma. Louis could tell she'd been crying. "What's the matter?" he asked, hoping it wasn't something *he* had inadvertently done to hurt her.

Joanna poured her heart out, telling Louis of the phone call from his angry dad. She began to cry again, apologizing for forgetting his mother's birthday.

Louis stood up and calmly walked across the room to the telephone. Without saying anything to Joanna, he punched out a number on the keypad.

"Hi, Mom, this is Louis," he said. Joanna held her breath.

"Listen, I'm *really* sorry I forgot your birthday. I hope you had a wonderful day yesterday anyway. I'll get you one of those belated cards as soon as I can. Hey, better late than never," Louis quipped, his voice light and warm. He paused.

"Can I speak with Dad?" Louis asked.

After a couple moments, Joanna heard Louis speak again. "Hello, Dad, this is Louis."

Joanna presumed that the pause signaled his dad's "hello" back.

"Dad," Louis continued with unmistakable precision, "I understand you called Joanna today about missing Mom's birthday. This was not hers to remember, and blaming her was wrong. I love you, Dad, but doing this is unacceptable. She's not your child; she's my wife. I expect you to never talk to her like that again."

Louis stopped talking. Joanna presumed that his dad was defending himself.

"No, sir," Louis broke in, his voice still calm and strong. "This is not up for discussion, Dad. Sorry."

Once again, Louis listened and then he spoke.

"I appreciate you saying that. Thanks for understanding. Good-bye, Dad."

For Louis and Joanna, this single conversation did more to short-circuit future in-law conflicts than years of therapy could have. What Louis did that day was to declare—to both his parents and his bride—where his primary loyalty would rest. And in doing so he created a sense of security for his wife. After that day she virtually never felt any competition with her in-laws. Louis's solidarity with her in their marriage was not in question.

The words of Scripture bear repeating: "A man will leave his father and mother and be united to his wife."[41]

I hope you never have to have this conversation with your dad. This transition from being your dad to the in-law in your marriage may be happening seamlessly. But if you ever face what Louis faced and don't take this kind of decisive action—if you fail to "leave" your primary loyalty to your parents to "be united" with your wife—you will be in serious trouble. Your neglect will put your bride and your parents—especially your mother—on a lifetime collision course. If you don't draw the line, these women will spend the rest of their lives competing for your affection.

"He's *mine*," one of them will say.

"No he's *mine*," the other will respond.

As cruel as it may sound, you have no choice but to choose your marriage over your loyalty to your parents. If you do what Louis did, you'll survive. If you don't—then let the games begin.

ESTABLISH CLEAR BOUNDARIES WITH YOUR OWN PARENTS

Growing up with an abusive alcoholic dad who eventually abandoned his family had an undeniable impact on Doug. And even though Doug's mom was devastated by her husband's behavior, she had sacrificed everything for her son's welfare. At times she was working three jobs in order to pay the bills.

And so when Doug's new wife, Lisa, began to experience some tension with her mother-in-law, Doug immediately sided with the woman who had always been his hero—his mother. Doug's mother often shared her "concerns about Lisa" with Doug. Because he loved and respected his mother so much, he believed that her advice, though not always presented in the most gracious terms, was given "for his own good."

Over the years, Doug tried to make subtle—and sometimes not so subtle—recommendations to Lisa about changes she should make in her habits, her behavior, or her personality. Increasingly, Lisa suspected that her husband was only parroting his mother's concerns. Lisa became more and more defensive, resisting even the slightest suggestions. And the icy intensity between Lisa and her mother-in-law began to bleed over into the marriage.

Doug knew he had to do something, so he stopped by Sam's office on his way home from work. Even though Sam was a few years older, there was a solid friendship between them—and Doug respected Sam's judgment.

In a few minutes, Doug asked a question that caught Sam's attention: "How can I get Lisa to make these reasonable changes my mother wants her to make?"

Sam's chair squeaked as he leaned back, folding his hands behind his head. "It sounds to me like you need to run away from home," Sam said, a gentle smile crossing his face.

Doug was shocked. "Run away from home?"

Then, from memory, Sam quoted, "For this reason a man will *leave* his father and mother and be united to his wife, and they will become one flesh." He continued on: "You've been trying to live in two homes, Doug. When you got married, you may have moved your possessions in with Lisa, but your heart is living somewhere else—it never left your mother. This is *your* deal, my friend—not Lisa's. Until you leave your mother and completely move in with Lisa, you're never going to get this fixed."

The sun had just disappeared on the horizon as Doug pulled into his driveway, but for him it was more like a sunrise. He was going to make a change. From now on, he had determined, whenever Lisa and his mother were on opposite sides of an issue—any issue—Doug was going to side with Lisa.

After a few weeks, Doug realized that his plan was going to be more difficult than he thought. At first, his mother was restrained about Doug's loyalty to Lisa. But when it became a consistent pattern, she became more vocal about it. Doug held his ground, which was even more difficult, because Lisa was still skeptical.

In the first two months, Doug's mother tried anger, tears, guilt—and even a surprise "intervention" and the reading of a twelve-page letter in Doug's office. Doug did his best to understand his mother's pain. Gently and lovingly, but without flinching, Doug explained to his mother that he *had* to leave home and emotionally move in with Lisa. Competing with Lisa was a battle his mom was going to lose.

Almost a hundred days after Doug's meeting with Sam, Lisa's shell began to crack. She overheard Doug on the phone with his mother. Lisa heard him defend her, sternly asking his mother to drop the subject. After months of commuting from his mother's home, Doug had finally run away.

We've seen many "Dougs" who dance between their mothers and their wives, hoping that they'll never have to declare primary loyalty to either one. These men have tried to coach their wives and placate their mothers. It never works.

During your first year of marriage, instead of attempting to negotiate a peaceful settlement between your mother—or your dad—and your wife, you be sure to let it be known that your primary loyalty will never be in question. *You will always side with your wife*. It's the only chance you have to save your wife's relationship with your parents.

EXES AND OTHER STRANGERS

Betsy and William were part of Mark and Susan's weekly marriage group. It was Betsy's second marriage, and because she had two boys from her first marriage, she still had regular contact with her ex. As the group talked about principles of healthy relationships with in-laws, Betsy spoke up, a look of new understanding sweeping across her face. "You know," she said, "it seems that a lot of these same principles work well for a relationship with an ex-spouse." Though some in the group laughed loudly, Mark could tell by her expression that she hadn't intended to be funny. He encouraged her to explain.

"I realized a long time ago," she continued, "that I have to move on and forgive my ex for whatever he's done to me. If I don't, I'm only holding myself hostage to bitterness. It's just like when a person can't forgive his parents or in-laws—they get stuck to the very people they're trying to get a healthy distance from."

Betsy had the group's undivided attention as she finished her comments: "When I keep myself tied to my ex-husband with a cord of resentment, it's almost impossible to keep the resentment from spilling over into my marriage as well."

Betsy was right. We cannot selectively harden our hearts with bitterness. The resentment seeps into our marriages, unintentionally poisoning them in the process.

THE HOLIDAY TUG-OF-WAR

If you haven't yet experienced the holiday tug-of-war, you will. And the entrance of your babies on the scene will intensify it. Here are a couple of things to remember about this game:

You and Your Wife Are In Charge

Thanksgiving and Christmas are the biggies. And in spite of the direct or indirect ways both sets of parents will use to try to influence your decisions, do not be controlled by these influences. With the full cooperation of your wife, decide what *you're* going to do.

Many couples alternate years—Thanksgiving with your parents this year and with hers next year. Some even it out by doing the same with Christmas, but making sure that Thanksgiving and Christmas are on alternating schedules—Thanksgiving with your family this year and Christmas with hers; then the other way around next year.

Some couples put the holidays on a three-year rotation, reserving the third year for themselves—something that will be even more important once you have kids of your own.

No Time for Surprises

Whatever you and your bride decide regarding holidays, don't keep your decision a secret from your families. Let them know well in advance. Surprises are a good idea under the Christmas tree, but letting everyone know where you'll be for the holiday celebrations shouldn't be one of them.

You may not want to make plans more than a year at a time, but keeping everyone in the loop when you finalize your plans will reduce the frustration of your parents' unfulfilled expectations.

PLANNED, YET FLEXIBLE; FAIR AND UNEQUAL

There will be times when, because of unusual circumstances such as a birth, serious illness, or death, you'll be tilting the balance of time toward one of your sets of parents. And because many couples live much closer to one set than to the other, it's virtually impossible that you'll be able to give equal time to each. Give up on that illusion, and issue each other a good deal of grace when this sort of inequality happens. So right now—before it happens—resolve that it will be okay. Unplanned events are traumatic enough without you and your wife fighting over "we've been spending a lot more time with your parents than we have with mine."

Be aware, too, that there may be good reasons to spend more time with one family over the other. We have discovered that women often need to spend more time with their families than men do. Of course, there are exceptions to this rule. Regardless, it's critical that you and your wife openly discuss your need to spend time with your own families, as well as any anxieties you may have about spending time with your spouse's clan.

Let's Make a Deal

In a counseling session with Mark, a frustrated Regina told her husband, Bruce, that she didn't appreciate his attitude when he was with her family. She explained to Mark that when they were with her parents, Bruce usually withdrew, often sticking his nose in a book or keeping his eyes glued to the television.

Once the issue was on the table, Mark challenged Bruce to make a simple commitment. "I promise to be totally present *and* pleasant to Regina's family for seven days a year," Bruce said, playfully raising his right hand. "She can choose the days, and she can count on me to be good."

Setting a boundary on the number of days eliminated the "be nice all the time" carte blanche that felt like a life sentence to Bruce. And it worked. In fact, Bruce's promise changed his attitude when he was with Regina's family. He really *did* have a better time.

Bring on a Baby

The chances are fairly slim that you'll have a baby in your first year of marriage, but it *does* happen. Most couples agree that the adjustments to pregnancy and the birth of their baby were far more significant than the alterations they went through when they got married.

When and if you have children, you're going to be an amateur dad, just like you were an amateur husband. Because the birth of your child changes your parents' status to a new unknown—grandparenting—they're going to go through adjustments, too. In fact, you'll begin hearing your parents say, "Well, when you were a baby, we did it this way." Remember to give them grace. Someday you'll do the same to your kids.

Again, as in all of your dealings with your parents and your in-laws, honor them but be your own man and listen carefully to your wife. Your marriage is your first priority; now so is your family. Your occasional friendly reminder of this to your parents will be a good idea.

"Mom," you might say, "I know you didn't breast-feed your babies, but Cindy's decided to go that route. And I support her."

"Dad, I know your heart was set on us naming our son after you," you might gently say to your father. "But we've decided to name him Amadeus. You know how much I love classical music."

Remember that it's *your* job to leave your parents' home. You've got a family of your own to establish. Gather as much advice as you need, but make your decisions confidently. To do otherwise is to invite chaos.

Oh, by the way, when that baby comes along, don't forget that the strength of your solid relationship with your wife will be the most important thing in your child's emotional health. When you walk in the door, in spite of the temptation to coo and fuss over the baby, greet your wife first. And don't be afraid to regularly invest in baby-sitters, so your bride will know that she's still number one. There may be times when you feel that you've lost your wife, that you can't possibly compete with a newborn baby for your wife's attention. During those times, be intentional about investing *with* her in the parenting process. Please notice I said *invest*. There's a handsome return on this investment!

REMEMBER, IN-LAWS ARE PEOPLE, TOO

Here's the good news about in-laws: They can be an incredibly important stabilizing factor in your marriage. In fact, in some European cultures, a low divorce rate is due, in large measure, to the presence of a supportive extended family that surrounds marriages with love and encouragement. Relationships with in-laws are healthiest when they avoid the extremes of enmeshment (overattachment) and isolation (overdetachment).

I began this chapter by confessing how it felt to become a father-in-law. How painful it was—even under the best of circumstances—to let my daughters go. There's no question I was guilty of insensitivity when I married Bobbie. I was presumptuously pitting a couple years of courtship against more than two decades of her parents' raising and nurturing her. They had sacrificed a lot more than I had, but I was "winning." I knew my marriage was more important than her relationship with her parents—and my relationship with my parents. But this was a huge adjustment for everyone.

I should have been more sympathetic. When I asked her dad for permission to marry her, he said, "Yes." But then—because I was living in Chicago and she was living in Washington D.C.—he added, "I'm sorry you're taking her so far away."

I said I understood, but it was a lie. I couldn't have possibly understood. But now I do, and someday many of you will, too.

Be gentle with your wife's parents. And don't be harsh with your own. These folks have loved you for a long time, and they really *do* want what's best for you. Whatever else they may be guilty of, in-laws are people, too.

12

HELP: WHEN SOMETHING'S GOT TO CHANGE

Marriage is a humbling journey.

BILL AND LYNNE HYBELS, *FIT TO BE TIED*

---◆◆◆---

C lint was a high-rolling businessman. Becky was his "trophy" wife. When they walked into a room together, everyone noticed. They owned whatever money could buy, but they were missing what it couldn't. She buried herself in civic clubs and raising her kids. He was seldom home, but when he was, his mind and heart were pre-occupied with the next big deal. She grew increasingly distant; he grew increasingly angry.

Before long, this father of two young children was entangled in an affair. In order to make his point, Clint didn't bother to hide anything, being seen in popular restaurants with his new flame. Though his mistress wasn't nearly as attractive as Becky, she was available with no strings attached—no demands, no expectations.

If you were to follow this true story through to the end,

where do you think it would lead? You'd probably assume that Clint eventually left Becky, who secured a crackerjack lawyer and took Clint to the cleaners. And you may think that there were months of a custody battle — with this messy divorce making for juicy gossip at all the cocktail parties in town for months. But you'd be wrong.

Here's how the story really ended: Today, over ten years after the affair, Clint and Becky are involved in a special ministry they began at their church. Every week they teach and counsel couples whose marriages are in trouble. (I'm not kidding. This is really happening.)

Clint and Becky stumbled into a healing process that many considered miraculous. And this same process — the one they now teach to young couples — if practiced early enough, can save any troubled marriage. In fact, it can save a marriage *before* it gets into serious trouble.

YOU MARRIED AN EXPERT

During the years when he carried a full counseling load, best-selling author Gary Smalley and his staff had the chance to have the following dialogue — or something close to it — with thousands of married couples.

> *Gary to the couple after hearing the details of their marital troubles:* "It sounds as though you've got some work to do."

> The couple nods.

> *Gary to the husband:* "So, Dave, what do you think you and Shelly need to do to fix these problems?"

> Complete silence. [Dr. Smalley and Dave's wife may as well have put their ears up to a conch shell. Except for a blank stare and slightly panicked

look, Dave says nothing. After a minute of silence,
Dave's stare drops to the floor in embarrassment.]
Gary to the wife: "Okay, Shelly, what do *you* think
you and Dave could do to fix your marriage?"

Shelly recaps some of the problems she and Dave are having and then offers a sequence of reasonable solutions. Gary
nods as Shelly is speaking. He's not surprised by her insight
and wisdom. Dave, on the other hand, *is* stunned and amazed.

The chances are better than 50/50 that Shelly and your wife
have something in common. (Truth be told, the odds are *much*
better than that.) Instinctively, intuitively, your wife is an expert
on these matters, including the relationship and the roles you
and she should take to ensure a successful marriage. And like a
mother bird protecting her nest from the attacks of the neighbor's cat, she's programmed to do whatever she can to safeguard
your marriage from all foes—big ones and little ones.

When you come home late for dinner or when you fail to
clean out the garage when you told her you would or when
you promise to spend more time with her and nothing comes
of it, your wife reacts. No, she overreacts. Why? Because she
knows that these "little" actions can signify the brewing of big
trouble, and she's going to call your attention to them. She's
going to do whatever she can to keep them from accumulat-
ing or growing. Small decisions of neglect can kill marriages.
Your wife knows it, which is why she tends to make big deals
out of little things.

LEARN TO RECOGNIZE EARLY WARNING SIGNS—
AND TAKE THEM SERIOUSLY

My flight was scheduled for 4:35 P.M., the last nonstop flight
of the day from Orlando to Los Angeles. At 4:10 there was no

effort to begin boarding passengers. I noticed the gate agent spending a lot of time on the phone. At 4:20, still no activity—no boarding.

"We're in trouble," I said just loud enough for the guy standing by me to turn and stare.

At 4:30 we got the announcement from the agent. "Ladies and gentleman," he said in his best be-calm-and-friendly voice, "we've received word from the flight crew that there is an indicator light on the instrument panel that is flashing a warning." There was an audible moan from the passengers in the waiting area. One young traveler tried to make a joke about how many pilots it takes to unscrew a lightbulb, but no one laughed.

"We've contacted a maintenance crew. Several diagnostics have been run. We're continuing to monitor the situation. We don't anticipate that this will result in a serious delay—perhaps twenty or thirty minutes—but we will keep you informed." Then he said my favorite five words of fiction—pure make-believe: "Thank you for your patience."

Some of the passengers began pacing back and forth; others spoke out in angry tones. Mothers fumbled through purses, looking for something new to keep their fidgety children occupied. I pulled out my cell phone and dialed the airline. I'd heard this "twenty or thirty minutes" story before.

A few minutes later I had a backup reservation for a connecting flight through Dallas. I had a critical meeting with a client the next morning in Los Angeles. Not getting there was not an option.

Nearly every time this happens to me, I wonder, *What are the chances that we'd still make it to Los Angeles if the captain really* did *go ahead and unscrew the warning light?* What do *you* think?

With all the redundant systems built into airliners, the chances are actually very good that we'd make it safely. In fact, if the crew members had kept their mouths shut, none of us would have even needed to know about the problem. We could have been obliviously munching on our pretzels and sipping ginger ale at thirty-five thousand feet if they had just overlooked it and let us board the plane. After all, *most* of the systems were working just fine.

But here's the truth: pilots can lose their privileges to fly if they ignore such things. They know that, even if the chances for serious trouble are minuscule, this indicator light *means* something. Impatient passengers or not, they're not going anywhere until they get it fixed. And getting broken things fixed immediately is just as important in your young marriage.

"What's wrong?" you say to your wife. You can tell something's bothering her.

"Nothing," she responds, her steely glare telling you that she's avoiding the light on the instrument panel.

You've probably already had this conversation.

What Clint learned as he recovered from his near-divorce experience with Becky—and what Dave learned as he listened to Shelly—was that early in their marriages there were plenty of warning lights they should have seen—lights their wives clearly saw. When it comes right down to it, most men admit that they *do* see them. They just choose to ignore them. *No marriage is perfect,* they foolishly rationalize. *We'll get over this in time.*

Call Maintenance

Pilots spend years in training. They prepare for the most horrific emergencies in simulators. Every time the wheels of their airplanes lift from the surface of the runways, pilots know that they alone hold in their hands the very lives of hundreds of trusting passengers. But pilots don't fix indicator lights. *They call maintenance.*

Admitting they need help is the part most men hate—and this loathing is almost universal. This habit shows itself most often in our inability—unwillingness, really—to stop and ask for directions. We're as lost as last year's Easter egg, we've passed the same 7-Eleven four times, our wife is crying (yelling) because we're late for a wedding, and we are *sure* that we're doing just fine.

"I know the church is right up here," we say with complete confidence.

Most marriages take off with no contingency plans on board. No one asks the question, "What will we do when a warning light goes on? How will we fix it, and who will we call if we can't fix it?" So a man takes off with no strategy for encountering trouble and with no understanding of how or whom to ask for help when he does run into problems.

As we've said, in most cases your wife has a better eye for warning lights than you do. Research has proven that women are more likely than men to raise concerns about their marriages.[42] But you and I are strangely comfortable with unscrewing the bulb (or smashing it with a hammer) and taking off for Los Angeles as though nothing is wrong. And the most tragic thing that can happen is that our flight lands without a hitch. Why? Because the experience of success simply proves to us that there must have been something wrong with the bulb instead of with the airplane. When our wives' warning lights go off, we've now got all the ammunition we need to convince ourselves that the only problem we've got is our wives and their overly sensitive warning systems.

One afternoon a minister's wife almost literally dragged her husband into the counselor's office. The first words out of the minister's mouth were, "I have no idea why we're here. We have a fine marriage." This man, professionally trained to counsel others, was completely blind to his own wife's desperate concerns.

During this first year of your marriage, you *must* keep your eye on the instrument panel. If you think you see something, ask your wife to confirm it. If the warning light is on, discuss the situation with her. Don't try to be funny. It's no place for a comedy routine. If you can't talk it through to the satisfaction of *both* of you, be sure to call maintenance.

"Maintenance" may be a trusted older friend, a minister, or a trained counselor. It's someone who will treat your warning light seriously.

Put Up a Safety Net

In January 1933, the construction of the Golden Gate Bridge in California began. Four-and-a-half years later, President Franklin Delano Roosevelt pressed a telegraph key in the White House, announcing to the world that the bridge was open.

During the construction of the bridge that cost thirty-five million dollars, only eleven workmen died. I say *only,* because the norm for construction like this was one man dead for every million dollars spent. The reason for the stellar safety record was very simple. The contractors invested a hundred thirty-five thousand dollars on a safety net that stretched under the bridge all the way from San Francisco to Marin County. As the bridge was being built, thirty men fell, but nineteen were caught in the net and saved. Local newspaper reporters dubbed the survivors "The Halfway to Hell Club."

A safety net under your marriage starts with an agreement to protect your marriage in the face of the dangers you're bound to encounter. And like the Geneva Convention in chapter 8, you and your wife must decide—right now, before you get into the heat of battle—that you will invest in this net.

Having this safety net also implies that you will lay down your weapons. You start building this safety net by agreeing never to employ armaments designed only to destroy and not to heal. Weapons like—

- defensiveness—"Oh, so it's all *my* fault now?"
- contempt—name-calling, cutting humor, or eye-rolling that accompanies such comments as, "So what're you going to do about it, sue me?"
- withholding attention—the impassive, non-responsive stone wall that moves you to a position of power by shutting down and not responding to your spouse at all.
- personal attacks—instead of asking your spouse to clean up her mess in the kitchen, you say, "You don't care about anyone but yourself, do you?"[43]

Using these weapons only escalates disagreements into arguments, arguments into fights, fights into a war, and a war into casualties—wounded or dead.

A safety net includes not only your promise that you'll not use these kinds of weapons but also a nonaggression treaty stipulating that the unarmed spouse always has the right to demand the laying down of one of these weapons the moment it appears.

"Hey, we promised not to do that," a spouse on the business side of the crosshairs may say. The weapon-toting offender must lay it down. They made a deal. He has no choice in the matter.

Another safety net may be a couple or a group of close friends who are on call in emergencies. One couple we know refers to these people as their "9–1–1 Group." They made a pact with each other that, day or night, they're available and willing to stand with each other and side with the marriage.

Randy and Tiffany created an explicit safety net early in their marriage. After they had been married for a few months and had faced the pain of nearly falling into "the San Francisco Bay" a few times, they sat at the kitchen table one evening after dinner. Randy pulled out his laptop, and together they made a list of things to include in their safety net. Because they were quite discerning, in addition to putting down some of the same kinds of safety-net emergency procedures described above, Randy and Tiffany added preventive measures of their own—things that would keep them from falling into the net at all.

Randy clicked away at his keyboard as Tiffany made her suggestions for him:

- A candlelight dinner once a month. Randy is responsible to execute it, even if he has to buy Chinese and transfer it from the cardboard containers to the good dinnerware.
- Conversations over coffee for fifteen minutes every weekday morning. Longer on weekends.
- Dance to "our" song or watch "our" video once a month.

Randy had a few of his own for Tiffany:

- Laugh when I try to be funny.
- Come to my business dinner parties.
- Initiate lovemaking.

As you read this, please avoid the temptation to roll your eyes and decide that making such lists is pure cheese. *I'm*

Mr. Spontaneity, you may be thinking. *I don't need to be so mechanical. I can make this stuff up as I go.*

Go ahead, but you're betting against the odds. The statistics are not on your side, unless you're hoping to join the "All the Way to Hell Club."

CAN WE TALK?

Hall of Famer Fran Tarkington, perhaps the best scrambling quarterback to ever run for cover, was presented with this riddle:

> Question: "What do life and a three-hundred-pound defensive lineman have in common?"
>
> Answer: "They both punish those who are unwilling to move."

If we amended this question just a little and put the word *married* in front of *life,* the answer would still be true. An unwillingness to adjust in *married life* will be punished.

You and I have this in common: we prefer not to have our faces slammed to the turf. We'll do almost anything to keep this from happening. Because you didn't know that a giant lineman would be turned loose in your marriage, you made no provisions to protect yourself before you walked the aisle. But since the day you and your bride got married, you've seen his massive form bearing down on you more than a few times.

Strangely enough, here's what this Leviathan might look like:

- How could you have known about her annoying little habits? How could she have *not* known about yours?

- You *thought* you saw her temper when you were dating, but it was nothing like this!
- She thought you liked her mother. You thought she liked your dad.
- You hate green paint. She loves green paint.
- He hates plaid fabric on furniture. You love plaid fabric on furniture.
- She tosses and turns at night like she's wrestling an alligator, while you lie perfectly still. Unfortunately, you're the light sleeper.
- She slams the kitchen cabinets when you're taking a nap in the family room.
- Dirt on a car is invisible to you. "Service engine soon" on the dashboard is invisible to her.
- Her morning breath would knock a fly off a manure spreader. You have gas and scratch yourself.[44]

Because you're new to your marriage, such things may be unfamiliar to you. Just wait. As inevitable as the sun's rising tomorrow and the Cubs still not making it to the World Series, these things—or others just like them—*are* going to happen. And when they do, what are you going to do about them? How are you going to deal with the angst that wells up in your gut when they show up?

You may have heard experts say, "A man can never change his wife." Or, "It takes two people to bring about change in a marriage." The experts are only half right. Countless husbands and wives have had a profound influence on each other. In other words, you *can* bring about changes in your wife. And here are three principles for success. The first one, in light of what I've just said, will surprise you:

Principle #1: Right from the Beginning, Give Up the Illusion of Changing Your Wife

This may be the hardest principle to grasp, because it seems to make no sense. "I thought you said I *can* change my wife. Now you're saying I should give it up?"

Exactly.

As ironic as it sounds, the first and most powerful step to take in changing your wife is to be intentional about *not* trying to change her at all. Whether it's her weight, the way she keeps the house, the way she always seems to be late, her reluctance to make love, or her habit of nagging you, the more you focus on changing her, the more frustrated both of you will become.

This woman you married is imperfect. Too many husbands are amazed and crushed by this discovery. So when this imperfection is exposed, some men use it to justify their rough behavior. You've probably heard a man rationalize and say, "But you don't understand the way she always . . ."

Some husbands make their wives into their number one home improvement project. So they become a veritable repository of "helpful" comments:

- "How much tonnage do you plan to put on this year?"
- "You talk too much."
- "When we got married, I never guessed I'd have to work so hard to get a little affection out of you."

If you ask these guys about their comments, they'll tell you that they're only trying to *help* their wives, or maybe even trying to make their marriages better. Their wives see it quite differently, of course.

In counseling, a husband can make what some call a "detailed confession of his wife's sins." Of course, he may add a surface confession of his own, such as, "Okay, I'll admit it. I'm not perfect either. But it isn't all my fault. And until she admits that she's had a part in this . . ." If this sounds more like a justification than a confession, it's only because you're paying attention.

It's easy to begin to let your love for your wife fade when your focus is on fixing her—not to mention that your attempts to change her will, in the long run, almost always fail. Even though there may be short-term behavior adjustments, your demands on her will just as likely have a "chemo effect." In your effort to remove the things you don't like, you can inadvertently kill some of the very qualities that attracted you to her in the first place.

Your pressure on her to "stop talking so much" can scrape the spontaneity from your "first love." Your constant oversight of her eating habits can create untold insecurity and low self-esteem. Your pressure on her to perform sexually can literally shut her spirit down.

When a man gets fixated on his wife's faults, the tragedy is that he forfeits his power to truly love her, which is the only way to ever bring about any real change in her. A man who is desperately trying to change his wife is actually in a tailspin of powerlessness. Change in your wife will always be a by-product of your love for her, not a result of direct and relentless demands.

Principle #2: Create an Environment in Which Change Will Happen

Your marriage is a living organism. It is at every moment either growing or dying. And growth always means change. Because you're wired to improve the woman you love, few things can be more disheartening than to feel that she's unaffected—no matter what you say or do.

Peter walked into Mark's office and slumped down in the chair in the corner. His body language spoke of a man who had just been whipped, but the happy look on his face spoke of something different. It was as though Peter had used all his physical energy to make the most important decision he had ever made about his new wife. His face reflected how pleased he was with the decision.

"I'm never going to criticize Katie again," he said to Mark.

Mark looked up from his desk, expecting an explanation. He knew of Peter and Katie's marriage—of the bitterness that swirled around it, of Katie's utter frustration with her judgmental husband. But in one sentence Peter had said to Mark all that he had come to say.

Six months later, Mark bumped into Katie at a church social. Her countenance was transformed. There was a sparkle in her eyes when Mark asked how she and Peter were doing. You see, when Peter made his promise, two things happened in his marriage: Katie began to trust him and feel safe around him, and, once she was convinced she wasn't being watched by a hall monitor and wouldn't be criticized, *she began to take the risk of making changes in her own behavior.*

A culture of change can never grow within a culture of criticism.

Try an experiment to see what I'm talking about. Ask your wife to stand and face you. Hold your hands up, palms facing her, and ask her to do the same, putting her palms against yours. Then slowly push against her hands. Without any instructions, her response to your pressure is completely predictable: She'll push back against your hands.

The last thing you and your wife want to do in your marriage is spend your years pushing against each other. Change is only possible when the pressure to perform is removed and then replaced with tenderness and grace.

Like a gardener who cannot force a seed to germinate, you can't force the little green shoot to sprout up but you *can* provide an environment that welcomes growth—one that encourages and then patiently waits.

Principle #3: Make the One Decision Most Likely to Bring About Change

Only two words: *Change yourself.* The most powerful thing you have in your toolbox for affecting change in your wife is to focus on the areas where *you* need to change.

When you do, you will begin to appreciate how hard it is to change ingrained patterns—and this will help you in the patience department. Next, bringing about even the smallest changes in yourself will keep you from feeling like a victim in your marriage—like you're powerless unless your wife changes. Finally, nothing will motivate your wife to change like being loved unconditionally by a man who is willing to change himself.

Here's an example of how this principle is broken: Suppose your wife has asked you to slow down when you're driving. She's asked you again and again. And suppose you choose to ignore her. In fact, when you're feeling particularly spunky, you defy her by punching the gas pedal the moment she says something. The result is that you're successfully establishing a no-change environment for your wife. And each time this—or something like it—happens, the ecosystem of your marriage grows increasingly rigid and inflexible.

Now here's an example of how this principle should work: Suppose your wife has asked you to slow down when you're driving. She's asked you again and again. And suppose that you slow down—extra credit for you, because you issue a sincere apology as you ease up on the gas pedal. You win. Your wife is no longer angry when you drive, and you've communicated your love for her in a very practical way. (By the way, have you seen the cost of speeding tickets these days?)

And here's something to celebrate: your wife wins too! She feels as though she *can* make a difference in your behavior. And, most important, your marriage wins, because the source of ongoing tension is removed. Because of what you've done, you begin to establish a pattern in which willing change is simply a demonstration of "the way we do things around here."

You go first, because your honest desire is to please your bride, *not* to manipulate her into doing the same. It's the *only* way your wife will make changes of her own.

WE INTERRUPT THESE DIVORCE PROCEEDINGS . . .

You may have heard the story of the man so filled with bitterness toward his wife that he decided a simple divorce proceeding would never do. So he went to his lawyer for advice on how to give his wife the most miserable divorce experience in the history of litigation. The man's lawyer came up with a brilliant plan.

"For the next thirty days," he said, "treat your wife with such unusual kindness that she'll begin to believe you *really* care about her. Then, when we issue the divorce papers, she'll be totally crushed."

The husband agreed that the suggestion was ingenious, and he set out to put the plan into action. For each of the next thirty days—

- he brought her a surprise gift
- he wrote her tender love notes
- he took her on dates to special places
- he listened to her advice respectfully and made appropriate adjustments in his own behavior

179

- he spoke with such kind words that he could have earned an Oscar for his performance—best supporting actor

Just before the thirty-day period expired, the man received a call from his lawyer. "The papers are ready for you to serve your wife," he said.

"Are you kidding?" the husband responded. "Forget the papers. My wife and I are having the time of our lives!"[45]

NOTES

1. "What Happens after the Wedding?" Interview with Pamela Paul, Sheryl Nissinen, and Terry Real (*The Oprah Winfrey Show*, air date: 28 October 2002); Sheryl Nissinen, *The Conscious Bride* (Oakland, Calif.: New Harbinger, 2000), 176.

2. John M. Gottman, *The Seven Principles for Making Marriage Work* (Three Rivers, Michigan: Three Rivers Press, 2000), 5.

3. Linda J. Waite and Maggie Gallagher, *The Case for Marriage: Why Married People Are Happier, Healthier, and Better-Off Financially* (New York: Doubleday, 2000), 67.

4. Ibid.

5. Ibid.

6. Cited in Philip Yancey, *Finding God in Unexpected Places* (Nashville: Moorings, 1995), 82.

7. Proverbs 21:9; 25:24.

8. Ephesians 5:25.

9. See the real-life examples in Les and Leslie Parrott, *Becoming Soul Mates* (Grand Rapids: Zondervan, 1995).

10. Deuteronomy 6:5, 7.

11. See 1 Corinthians 12:3–6.

12. Philippians 2:7.

13. The Green River is known around the world as one of the most dangerous on a river raft. Years ago, a very popular Pepsi advertisement featured a raft full of adventurers on this very river!

14. Ephesians 5:25.

15. See Gary Chapman, *The Five Love Languages* (Chicago: Northfield, 1992).

16. It's no surprise that some Bible translations describe sexual intercourse by using the word *know*—as in, "And Adam knew Eve his wife; and she conceived, and bare Cain" (Genesis 4:1 KJV).

17. Chris Fabry, *Focus on the Family Magazine* (February 1999), 3.

18. Among Charlie Shedd's best-selling classics were *Letters to Karen* and *Letters to Phillip*.

19. Charlie took the old adage to heart: "If Mama ain't happy, ain't nobody happy."

20. The Holter monitor is a twenty-four-hour continuous recording of a person's electrocardiogram (ECG). It permits recognition of any rhythm changes of the heart that may occur during daily activities.

21. For more information, see Gottman, *Seven Principles for Making Marriage Work*.

22. Gottman, *Seven Principles for Making Marriage Work*, 17, 20.

23. For his efforts in beginning the process that resulted in the Geneva Convention, Henri Dunant received the Nobel Peace Prize in 1901. Inspired by the lives of three remarkable women—Harriet Beecher Stowe, Florence Nightingale, and Elizabeth Fry—Henri Dunant wrote, "The influence of women is an essential factor in the welfare of humanity, and it will become more valuable as time proceeds." He was also the founder of the International Committee of the Red Cross.

24. 1 Peter 3:7.

25. Colossians 3:19.

26. Mark DeVries and I do not pretend to be experts regarding your personal finances. There are, however, many helpful books written by Larry Burkett, Ron Blue, and David Ramsey—as well as a number of excellent classes you can take at your church (the ones produced by Crown Ministries, for example).

27. My favorite is QuickBooks.

28. Proverbs 22:7.

29. In most court settlements, a couple's money is treated as "theirs," not "his" or "hers." It's the court's opinion that the money is yours together, and it's a good idea for you to think of it this way, too.

30. Acts 20:35 (THE MESSAGE).

31. 1 Timothy 6:10.

32. I develop this in greater detail on pages 35–38 in *She Calls Me Daddy* (Colorado Springs: Focus on the Family, 1996).

33. If you could use some playground suggestions, here are a few: Bathe together by candlelight, give each other a body massage with scented oil, take a buggy or sleigh ride together, take ballroom dancing lessons, go look at newborn babies in the hospital (this one's huge, trust me!), have a picnic in the country, swing on the swings at a playground, plan a secret rendezvous, have a water-pistol fight, pray on your knees, or watch the stars.

34. I could tell you about breast pumps at this point, but I'll not do it. Some of you may learn about them soon enough.

35. Cited in Dennis Rainey, *Family Reformation* (Little Rock, Ark.: Family Life, 1996), 94.

36. Cited in Peter Blitchington, *Sex Roles and the Christian Family* (Wheaton, Ill.: Tyndale House, 1985), 165.

37. Jerry Jenkins has written a wonderful book about this subject called *Loving Your Marriage Enough to Protect It* (Chicago: Moody Press, 2000).

38. I strongly recommend the book *Every Man's Battle* by Stephen Arterburn and Fred Stoeker, with Mike Yorkey (Colorado Springs: WaterBrook, 2000).

39. The authors of *Every Man's Battle* call this idea "the bounce." Your eyes, like a rubber ball, "hit" the subject and then bounce away. They do not go back for another look—a very good idea!

40. Orel Hershiser, with Robert Wolgemuth, *Between the Lines* (New York: Warner Books, 2001), 144.

41. Genesis 2:24.

42. See Gottman, *Seven Principles for Making Marriage Work*, 114.

43. John Gottman notes some of these ideas in his book *Why Marriages Succeed or Fail* (New York: Simon & Schuster, 1994).

44. One of the reasons couples choose to live together before they get married is to avoid being surprised by these annoyances after they're married. However, couples who decide to live together before they're married are statistically *more* likely to divorce than those who wait until they're married before living together. Cited in Pamela Paul, *The Starter Marriage* (New York: Villard Books, 2002).

45. Adapted from a story in Neil Clark Warren, *Catching the Rhythm of Love* (Nashville: Nelson, 2000), 28–30.

Couples of the Bible

A One-Year Devotional Study of Couples in Scripture

Robert and Bobbie Wolgemuth

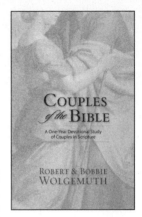

In this scrapbook of your spiritual family tree faithful patriarchs and matriarchs who make you proud . . . and scoundrels you'd rather not talk about. But all of these couples of the Bible will give you a instructive snapshot of your biblical heritage. Some bring encouragement; others offer a stern warning.

Through this 52-week devotional experience, you will be reacquainted with the challenges and outcomes of familiar couples such as Abraham and Sarah . . . and meet some lesser-known couples such as Othniel and Aksah. Each week focuses on one couple, from Adam and Eve to Christ and His Bride. You will read their story, learn about their cultural setting, and explore how their story can teach important truths about your own marriage. You will be guided with questions to help you apply biblical truth to your relationship with your spouse. And you'll finish the week with a time of reflection, thanksgiving, and prayer.

Couples of the Bible will teach you how God guided couples in the past and will encourage you to trust in his faithfulness for your marriage both in the present and in the future.

Men of the Bible

A One-Year Devotional Study of Men in Scripture

*Ann Spangler and
Robert Wolgemuth*

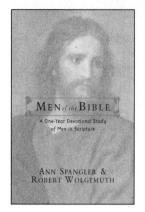

Men of the Bible offers both men
and women a fresh way to read and
understand the Bible—through the
eyes and hearts of the men whose stories unfold in its pages.
This unique book takes a close-up look at fifty-two men in
Scripture whose dramatic life stories provide a fresh perspective on the unfolding story of redemption.

Though our culture differs vastly from theirs, the fundamen-
tal issues we face remain the same. We still reach for great
dreams and selfish ambitions. We wrestle with fear and indeci-
sion and experience the ache of loneliness and the devastation
of betrayal. And, like many of these men, we long to walk more
closely with the God who calls us into an intimate relationship
with himself.

In *Men of the Bible*, each week becomes a personal retreat
focused on the life of a particular man: His Story—a narrative re-
telling of the biblical story; A Look at the Man—focusing on the
heart of the man and how his story connects with your own life;
His Legacy in Scripture—a short Bible study on principles revealed through his life; His Legacy of Promise—Bible promises
that apply to his life and yours; His Legacy of Prayer—praying
in the light of his story.

Women of the Bible

A One-Year Devotional
Study of Women in
Scripture

*Ann Spangler and
Jean E. Syswerda*

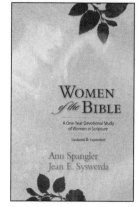

Women of the Bible, by Ann Spangler
and Jean E. Syswerda, focuses on
fifty-two remarkable women in Scripture—women whose
struggles to live with faith and courage are not unlike your
own. The women in this book encourage you through their
failures as well as their successes.

Women of the Bible offers a unique devotional experience
that combines five elements. Each week becomes a personal
retreat focused on the life of a particular woman: Her Story—a
moving portrait of her life; Her Life and Times—background information about the culture of her day; Her Legacy in
Scripture—a short Bible study on her life; Her Promise—Bible
promises that apply to her life and yours; Her Legacy of Prayer—
praying in the light of her story.

Special features include a list of all the women of the Bible,
a timeline of the women of the Bible, a list of women in Jesus'
family tree, and a list of women in Jesus' life and ministry

This yearlong devotional will help you slow down and savor
the story of God's unrelenting love for his people, offering a fresh
perspective that will nourish and strengthen your personal com-
munion with him.

Share Your Thoughts

With the Author: Your comments will be forwarded to the author when you send them to *zauthor@zondervan.com*.

With Zondervan: Submit your review of this book by writing to *zreview@zondervan.com*.

Free Online Resources at
www.zondervan.com

Zondervan AuthorTracker: Be notified whenever your favorite authors publish new books, go on tour, or post an update about what's happening in their lives at www.zondervan.com/authortracker.

Daily Bible Verses and Devotions: Enrich your life with daily Bible verses or devotions that help you start every morning focused on God. Visit www.zondervan.com/newsletters.

Free Email Publications: Sign up for newsletters on Christian living, academic resources, church ministry, fiction, children's resources, and more. Visit www.zondervan.com/newsletters.

Zondervan Bible Search: Find and compare Bible passages in a variety of translations at www.zondervanbiblesearch.com.

Other Benefits: Register yourself to receive online benefits like coupons and special offers, or to participate in research.